OCCASIONAL
therapy™

FOR YOUR MIDLIFE YEARS

12

SESSIONS TO

COMBAT YOUR CRISIS

DR. ELLYN GAMBERG, Ed. D

ELLIS & YOUNG PUBLISHING.
NEW YORK, NEW YORK

Library of Congress Cataloging-in-Publication Data is available upon request.

0-9802493-1-7
978-0-9802493-1-6

10   9   8   7   6   5   4   3   2   1

Designed by Pauline Neuwirth, Neuwirth & Associates, Inc.

Printed in the United States of America

Distributed by Midpoint Trade Books

"The purpose of life is not to be happy. It is to be useful, to be honorable, to be compassionate, to have it make some difference that you have lived and lived well."

—RALPH WALDO EMERSON

"There is a fountain of youth: it is your mind, your talents, the creativity you bring to your life and the lives of people you love. When you learn to tap this source, you will truly have defeated age."

—SOPHIA LOREN

ACKNOWLEDGMENTS

I AM THANKFUL FOR the years spent during the *first half of my life* joyfully watching my children grow; and I wish them the same joy as they watch me now blossom during *the second half of my life*. This second journey would not be complete without my husband by my side. He applauds the person I have been; and reminds me that I am only half way to becoming the person I was meant to be.

I am grateful to my editor, Trish, who along with lessons in grammar, shared laughter, insight, and a little bit of herself. All of which made the words come alive. I appreciate Pauline's eye for design, her candid comments, and perpetual patience. I am fortunate for the *second chance* to work with Eric and his team.

I am honored that my colleagues, Geri and Sandor, recognize the importance of my work; and have graciously contributed valuable time and expertise.

CONTENTS

INTRODUCTION

W<small>E ALL KNOW</small> the stereotype . . . the fifty-year-old guy who wakes up one day and buys a new sports car, dyes his hair, and gets a girlfriend half his age (and half his wife's weight). Or the woman who starts dressing like her twenty-year-old daughter, opts for liposuction, and has a fling with her neighbor (also, half her age—and half her husband's weight—*thank you*). These images are part of our culture—we see them on TV and in movies, and in the guy down the street, the one we snicker about behind his back.

But when it comes to ourselves, when those first early warning signs of midlife show up, we often barely notice them . . . or at least we do our best to ignore them.

And who could blame us? You may find yourself squinting to read the morning paper (no problem, just extend your arm a little). Or perhaps you catch sight of yourself in the mirror one day, and barely recognize yourself because the extra pounds are catching up with you (it's the shirt, you tell yourself.) For others, it is those increasing numbers of gray hairs that are gradually taking over your head. (Dad went gray earlier than me, *I'm doing OK*, you kid yourself.)

Your feelings may be reaching into a lot of gray areas, as well. Many people at midlife feel that their life has reached some weird, suspended state—overcome by vague feelings of loss and change: you lose your youthful looks, you "lose" the children you have raised (as they move off to college or away from home), you change your life activities, and a hundred other reasons. You know that you're not young anymore, but you're definitely not old . . . *right?* Likewise, stepping into other new roles—as caretaker of your aging parents, the new grandmother/father, etc.—while wonderful, may be completely confusing. All of which lead you to say *is this all there is? What have I done with my life?*

Obviously, the tumult you have been feeling may be affecting your relationships, as well. Many middle-age women—who aren't immune to the midlife crises—may insist on more "equality" with their husbands now that the kids are gone. But this may be in part to cover up the fact that you are losing your primary role in life: as mother. And your emergence as an independent and free woman can strain even the healthiest of marriages. Likewise, both of you may already be reevaluating your relationship—which can yield anything from feelings of boredom to feeling trapped or, quite simply, "I've had enough."

And if we don't notice the changes, those around us most certainly do. "Mom, you're old," is enough to make most women cry (as if with those hormones you actually need something to make you cry). Similarly, for men, the first time that their kids catch them in a less-than-flattering light can be equally humbling.

Kids, as always, bring their own unpredictable dynamic. You are probably alternating between feeling happy they are gone to missing their presence around the house every day. Younger boomers may be borrowing their jeans (yech, *mom!*) or trying to be their buddy.

At least you can get away from all of this at work, right? *Fat chance.* Particularly given our downsizing, consolidating, outsourcing way of life, all those youthful recruits (with their fresh faces and natural hair color), may be making you feel that you are not on the way up—but the way out. To counter that, many boomers become the Devil in Prada. After all, you must prove to the boss, your coworkers, and anyone else who will listen (usually, no one) that you are still "in charge" and need to be respected.

Relationship-wise, emotions are not the only issue. Women are certainly having physical shifts: hormones changing, and—depending upon their age—dealing with the loss of reproductive capabilities, or, increasingly, having a child in their forties. Men may be having their own sexual issues . . . so it becomes Viagra meets menopause—and then what? No wonder our kids are telling us we're old.

For some of you, relationships with your children might go beyond strained to just plain unhealthy. Some, who don't let go when they ought to, impede their children's adult independence, and consequently, hamper their own post-parenting lives. (Hint: When you think of your kids' successes and failures as your own and thus try to immunize your child against failure, you might be one of an increasingly growing number of a new, boomer phenomenon: the "perma-parents.") But not only is this not emotionally healthy for your children—really, there is life after a B+ grade—you may be setting yourself up for a big letdown after they (undoubtedly) go in their own direction.

Of course, much of the whirlwind of emotions you are facing may be, in no small part, because of that ultimate issue no one wants to think about—death. At some point, all of us feel the weight of moving past the halfway point, or what we perceive to be that point, in our lives. For some, it comes in the form of a parent's death, or the passing away of a friend or relative. By now most of us have already experienced the loss that comes with the death of a loved one; and for many of us, at some point, the possibility of death becomes an increasingly conscious presence.

And how, exactly, are you feeling lately? Depressed, anxious, tired, or irritable; perhaps you're not sleeping enough or losing concentration—and it's beginning to affect your behavior at work, or socially. When it gets to be too much, you may even begin to hide your sadness, by self-medicating, seeking some "feel-good" antidotes, or just feeling anger, sadness, and guilt over nothing in particular. You may feel trapped and that you have lost a sense of who you are. And while perhaps you've never been so aware of the nuances at play in all of your many relationships—at the same time, you've felt more isolated and alone. Suddenly, buying that sports car . . . or having that fling, telling off the boss at work—or whatever represents escape to you—is starting to make sense.

So, What Is Going Wrong Here?

Traditionally, midlife has been known as a period of loss: declining looks, a loss of reproductive capacity, physical strength, economic status, security, and a diminishing social network. You have worked hard for decades to build a stable home, create and nurture a family, develop a career, keep in good shape—and suddenly—everything seems to be changing (and rarely for the better). Although, technically speaking, you don't feel old—these sudden changes make you feel as though you are living in someone else's body.

"Midlife" is such a big deal, because—whether we know it or not—we are all wired to see life in two stages. The first half of life, generally speaking, focuses on the development of a personality and building a sense of self (which is called the ego).

This first phase of life involves utilizing the skills and abilities you have been given (or, at least, you believe you possess) so you can survive and prosper. The second half of life involves finding those hidden talents and desires that often become buried under the everyday laundry of life and putting them together with all the wisdom and experience you have acquired about yourself. Hopefully you come up with a unified, happy person. The passageway of midlife joins the first and the second halves of life. Midlife is the place of transition and transformation.

So why, then, can midlife be so stressful for so many of us?

No matter what midlife throws at us—and I know that, at times, it can be a lot—it is necessary to reflect on where you have been in order to see clearly where you are going. All of us, even the most "well adjusted," can use midlife to focus on becoming who we were meant to be rather than who we think others want us to be. Midlife is a time to examine and evaluate every aspect of your life and search for deeper meaning. And actually, now that the kids are out of the house, we do have a lot more time on our hands. . . .

That's Great: Everyone Goes Through This . . . But What Can I Do About It?

By the time you are finished reading this book, you should be able to see—even if it's with the help of your bifocals—that midlife is a period of opportunity. The wisdom you have gained and the freedom that comes from no longer putting the needs of others first can create a new and wonderful independence. Midlife is not the end of the line, or the end of life. It is not your retreat into retirement. You will only be tossed on the side of the road if you let yourself be. The midlife years are the time for reinvention. It can be a time when women—and men—can shape their lives without all of the "should" that may have constrained them earlier. For those with grown children, as well as for those who have not had children, you need to find new ways to nurture and thrive. . . .

Occasional Therapy for Your Midlife Years will give you the direction and drive you need. In the pages to come, you will find plenty of inspiration. You will be able to look in the mirror and see something beautiful again. You will be able to change the lens through which you view life, graciously saying goodbye to your past life, and welcoming the new one waiting for you just around the corner.

Although you may not have all the skills you need to cope right now (stay with me, you will soon enough), we do have control over how we react, how we respond, and how we feel about ourselves. And yes, really, we are responsible only for own behavior and own our own feelings. We cannot change the cycle of time—but this particular phase of life does afford all of us more time to work on ourselves.

We all seem to know when a cold is coming on and take immediate action to prevent it from getting worse: we crawl into bed, call in sick to work, and cancel our evening plans. But when we become mentally exhausted or sick over a day's events, we keep going, hoping that the condition will just go away on its own. And of course we know it won't. Dealing with a looming lifecycle transition—like midlife—takes work; but not as much as you may think when you have a simple, clear plan of action. Sound interesting? Keep reading.

Occasional Therapy: The Key to Changing How You Think About Midlife

Occasional Therapy is for those people who need help on occasion. It is an eclectic approach to helping people, like you, who are otherwise well adjusted but are facing a difficult or troubling situation or time in their lives. *Occasional Therapy* combines the most powerful parts of a wide variety of therapeutic techniques. The exercises, techniques, and approaches presented in this book will allow you to become an active participant in your mental well-being and how you deal with the uneasiness you are feeling. The best part about *Occasional Therapy* is that you will start learning strategies—today—that can help you *before* you need them. This book will allow you to work at your own pace, in the privacy of your own home. *Occasional Therapy* is *not* about spending endless amounts of time revisiting childhood problems. It *is* about learning clear, simple strategies to help you deal with the issues you are facing today.

Would you like to master an easy-to-use exercise that will have you slowing down the rhythm of your body—the hurried breaths, and the chatter in your head, eliminating all the negative thoughts, worries, and "what ifs" running rampant in your mind—and be able to harness this ability whenever you want? (Great, you will find exactly that in Chapter Four.) Or, how about some suggestions that you can use—now—to find the real reason you and your spouse are no longer truly connecting? (No problem—turn to Chapter Six.) *Occasional Therapy* will have you engaging in thoughts and verbal interactions that bring about self-knowledge and achieve clarification of feelings; it has been specifically created to alter behaviors and create improved interpersonal skills.

If you thought that reading this book would involve months or years of your time, or meant dredging up painful memories, would you be reading this right now? I thought not. Actually, reading *Occasional Therapy for Your Midlife Years* and utilizing the strategies taken from short-term therapy models may be the best hope in reaching people like you: ones who really need help—now! The brief psychotherapy techniques offered in *Occasional Therapy* seek to empower you while generating a few simple solutions. Reading *Occasional Therapy* will maximize the limited amount you have to work at it through the easy-to-use, clear strategies that I provide throughout the book. You will not hear endless anecdotes or cute stories about other peoples' lives. I know that you are reading the book to help yourself, and *Occasional Therapy* was written with you in mind.

While the term "Occasional Therapy" is new, the theories that led to its development are not. *Occasional Therapy* is based on theories of cognitive behavioral therapy, a school of therapy that attempts to help people by modifying everyday thoughts and behaviors. Treatment is generally brief, time-limited, and focused on the problems linked directly to the immediate stressor.

Occasional Therapy, like other forms of short-term therapy, is for people going through some change in their life, who are searching for a level of balance or acceptance with the environment, others, or themselves. *Occasional Therapy*, like short-term therapies in general, is a time-tested, respected approach to dealing with the stark realities of situational events.

You Are Not Alone

Occasional Therapy for Your Midlife Years is meant to be a resource for people, like you, who are hesitant to seek therapy, know they need help, and want to help themselves—if they only had the tools. You should take comfort in knowing that many of life's transitional events (and the associated feelings and behaviors) are "normal," and that—more importantly— you are not alone. The topics in this book may be general, but the issues are very personal. Many of these topics are things that people think about constantly but don't talk about with anyone out of fear or out of embarrassment, feeling uncomfortable, etc. Reading this book can help provide the help-and-security you need.

Occasional Therapy will also help you appreciate how the events of our lives are interrelated. You may be focused on your own aging—so much so that you fail to realize how much your marriage is suffering; perhaps you are so obsessed with your troubled marriage that your career is left by the wayside. Whatever the case, we often become so obsessed with one issue that we fail to see (or we deny) that it has spilled into other areas of our life. Sometimes, the connections may be so subtle that we hardly know they are there; but the different areas of our life do not exist in a vacuum.

One major benefit of reading *Occasional Therapy for Your Midlife Years* is perhaps less "selfish." This book will provide insights into what others are going through, what they are thinking and feeling, and how you can help them, and yourself. While you may benefit from this book if you yourself are going through a difficult time, it can be just as helpful in understanding someone you love. In a society that is all about "ME," reading this book gives you the opportunity to reach out and connect with others on a more personal level. In many cases, working out issues together—or just being supportive—improves relationships and at the same time solves individual problems. In short, everyone wins.

Please note: *Occasional Therapy for Your Midlife Years* offers strategies, exercises, and suggestions regarding specific problems—in particular, the many "lifecycle events"—such as dealing with our kids moving away from home, facing retirement, or issues at work (to name a few) that we all experience. Reading *Occasional Therapy* will also be helpful if you wonder if your particular situation and reactions to it are normal. Participating in individual psychotherapy may be better for you if you want to understand your patterns of behavior and how they developed, or if you have had repeated difficulties with family and work relationships, that have significantly impaired your social or occupational ability to function. Seeking help from your own mental health care professional is absolutely essential if you are suicidal, psychotic, or suffer from a condition requiring medication.

Discover the Power That Comes With a New Perspective

When confronted with a difficult situation, most people will automatically draw upon past experiences when responding. Our past experiences, emotions, or situations have become the basis for patterns of behavior that we repeat over and over again—whether or not they work.

But what about the decisions required by a completely new experience, like those of becoming an in-law, having your first grandchild, or having to retire? When faced with a challenging new situation—or an unfamiliar emotion for which you have no past frame of reference—you will probably become uncomfortable and (like most of us) feel the need to share our pain or confusion with a loved one. You may turn to a friend, parent, significant other, sibling, or other trusted love one for advice or comfort. Yet too many times, it is these same people who are involved in the troubling situation. Or they may have little or no experience dealing with the situation. (If you've recently called your sister—who's sworn off marriage and children—for her advice on dealing with your kids, you know what I mean here.)

Reading *Occasional Therapy for Your Midlife Years* will allow you to focus on yourself without the distraction of others' opinions, criticisms, or judgments. The supportive, therapeutic suggestions made here will provide you with the freedom needed to look inside yourself and discover your own insights and solutions. Through experience, I have found that most people who are determined to resolve the issues for which they seek professional help are capable of resolving their own problems. You are no different.

What's That . . . Botox May Not be the Answer

Our world today is so fast-paced and frenetic that we often lose sight of what truly is important. Busy with our own individual expectations, with family pressures, work demands, financial burdens, and everything else—particularly around stressful life events—our lives become overrun with confusion, conflict, frustration, and disappointment. Since we have become conditioned to instant gratification, and are pressured by the time crunch, and are used to a whole host of everyday time-saving conveniences, we want our problems fixed in the same way (i.e., yesterday). Yet, tending to our personal well-being and health often comes last on our list, if at all; even something as simple—and vital—as a regular physician checkup becomes a hassle. As much as we may need it, engaging in weeks of psychotherapy may not be practical.

It is not surprising given the harrowing pace of our daily lives, that we have conned ourselves into thinking that just about anything can be emotionally beneficial. The once exclusively clinical term "therapy" has morphed into something else over the last few decades. We now refer to anything that makes us feel better as therapy—"shopping therapy," "chocolate therapy," "spa therapy"—you get the idea. Are these helpful? Sure. But they won't address the real, underlying issues affecting you. *Occasional Therapy* is therapy for today: it strikes a balance between the realities of our need-it-yesterday world and the necessity of finding *real* solutions that produce long-term, tangible results.

I Know Why I'm Reading This,
But Why Do You Advocate Occasional Therapy?

As a mother who has raised three children, packed them off to college, walked them down the wedding aisle, and worked hard at a career and marriage, I found myself looking around my empty nest and reflecting on all those past transitions and events that I had survived (some definitely more easily than others). As a clinician for twenty-five years, I had come home from work every day after listening to the anxiety and stress of patients transitioning through their own lifecycle events (be it career troubles, romance issues, the death of a loved one, you name it). I began to realize that we all face the same things and that everyone (even psychologists, psychiatrists, and psychotherapists) will face challenges and changes that can be difficult. As I developed the concept of *Occasional Therapy* and began to successfully use it with my clients—and tried it on myself—I realized cognitive behavioral therapy could be useful for people in most transitional and major lifecycle events.

These days, we seem to have a difficult time figuring out what is really "normal." Our society has so many variations and definitions of what is socially acceptable, politically correct, etc., that it becomes difficult to make sense of our own feelings and behaviors. Additionally, the need for acceptance from friends, family, and coworkers forces us to create a personal mask that sometimes hides our inability to effectively cope with what are "normal events" in our lives. In writing *Occasional Therapy for Your Midlife Years*, I wanted people to feel that they are not alone, and that if others can be helped, so can they. Reading this book will create an avenue for privacy for exploring the personal, intimate issues that you have wondered about, but did not want to share with others.

How to Use This Book

You will find this book to be enjoyable to read and easy to use. It will help you learn how to ask—and answer—the questions that are bothering you now. *Occasional Therapy for Your Midlife Years* provides exercises, strategies, and techniques you can start using now, and it allows you to take an active role in your own psychological growth. This book is divided into chapters addressing some of the major life events. Of course, you will want to read those chapters that apply to you now. You might want to read ahead to sections that are in the near future for you, as well. And you *should* read the chapters on issues your loved ones are facing so that you can better understand their thoughts, problems, and, of course, how they are affecting you.

You may find that it's helpful to keep a notebook on hand to jot down your own personal notes along the way. Each chapter begins with some *background* and then quickly moves to *symptoms* (you know, the reasons you picked up this book in the first place). In *Presenting Problems*, the deeper issues most likely bringing about those symptoms are discussed in detail. Throughout the "Problems" section, I offer techniques that you can begin using now, alone, or with your partner, parents, siblings, or a friend. I don't pretend to have all the answers to every question; not every problem or issue has a corresponding exercise, and some have several. And that's exactly the point: you will see that with *Occasional Therapy*, sometimes the best exercise is to simply be *aware* of the issue. And at the end of each chapter, I have included some *insights*, *my* thoughts assembled after twenty-plus years of doing this.

Most importantly, you will learn about your own behaviors and how you can actively change them when faced with events in your life. Reading *Occasional Therapy for Your Midlife Years* will help you figure out how to survive midlife—and how to begin seeing it as a period of possibilities and transformations, not just restrictions.

So, what's next? Set aside some time and find a quiet place that is yours alone. Get comfortable in your favorite chair and relax your mind and your body. Read carefully and enjoy at your own pace. You are closer than you think to facing midlife head-on, with a sense of calm and the belief that you are in control of your emotions, feelings, and future.

1

STILL YOUNG AT HEART

So What Exactly

Is *Middle Age?*

~

*I*F YOU DIDN'T know how old you were, how old would you be? I know that some mornings you may feel like you are ninety, and other days you feel that fifty-five is now "the new twenty-one." Age and time are confusing principles to understand, and for many of us, this is never more obvious than during middle age.

However, we can all agree that "middle age" is that period of life after young adulthood but before the onset of old age. Most attempts to define middle age place it at the third quarter of the average lifespan, but there is quite some leeway here. The preeminent developmental psychologist Erik Erikson saw middle age as covering a wide range, defining middle adulthood as between 40 and 65. The U.S. Census (2006) lists middle age as including only the age categories 35 to 44 and 45 to 54. *(So then, our senior years begin at 55?)* Likewise, most people in their midlife years consider themselves as "young" and of course, as "adults." However, they're far from being *young adults* and will also will sneer at any mention that they are heading anywhere near "old age."

On those mornings when you're feeling closer to ninety, you may believe that middle age is a somewhat nebulous—but ever-growing—list of physical symptoms: that curious loss of elasticity to your skin or the blotches that seem to pop up everywhere; strength that isn't quite what it used to be, and there is that expanding waistline. And in case you're not seeing it for yourself, the media sure will kindly help you outwit aging with a never-ending parade of anti-aging, youth-retaining products, creams, lotions, and medicines.

However, defining middle age solely by physical symptoms—as the woman who hates her neck or the guy who despises his thinning hair may be tempted to do—is kidding ourselves, because those changes hit each of us at different times, and with very different effects. Many women are never bothered by menopause and lots of men don't turn gray until their 60s; more women are having children (and by natural childbirth) into their early 40s, and we all have friends—of both sexes—who are in better physical health now than they were twenty years ago. So then, defining middle age by its associated physical changes is not enough: these changes arrive for each of us at different times, in a wide range of varieties—and elicit such a range of responses.

What about all the *issues* that accompany midlife—all of the emotional, career-related, marriage, children, and family issues that may come to define, and sometimes overrun, our middle years? In our country, as in most Western societies, middle age is thought to be the stage of life in which a person is expected to have "settled down" in terms of their sense of identity and place in the world. But for every person facing insecurity and guilt, another is able to tackle life head-on. And for every person laid-off or outsourced, another enjoys a promotion, opens up his own business, or just enjoys retirement. We can choose to define middle age as simply turmoil with the kids, or the spouse—but for each of us besieged with problems in these arenas, another has only limited troubles or none at all.

Instead, I propose that we can define

middle age by looking at what it is not:

the very young or the very old.

HOW OLD ARE YOU REALLY?

Read through the following checklist of common Physical, Emotional, and Cognitive Signs and Symptoms of Aging. Circle those things that you notice have changed in the last few years, or months, or since yesterday.

SECTION ONE: Physical

1. Clothes don't seem to fit as well
2. Weight "shift"—you weigh the same, but the pounds have transferred to different parts of your body
3. Displeasure with weight, hips, legs, thighs, and stomach (or your entire body)
4. Hot flashes that keep you (and your partner) up at night
5. Difficulty reading the small print on the menu or on the label
6. Excessive attention to your balding hair or graying hair

SECTION TWO: Emotional

1. A sense of loss and emptiness now that the kids are gone
2. Feeling depressed or discouraged about aging
3. An overwhelming sense of responsibility for your aging parents (and everyone else)
4. Tired, burned out, overworked, and underappreciated
5. Searching for something (or someone) new and better to make your life complete

SECTION THREE: Cognitive

1. Trouble recalling where you put the keys, or the name of the receptionist at the doctor's office
2. Finding that it takes you a little longer to get through the crossword puzzle, or to learn the new features on your cell phone
3. Slower hand-eye coordination
4. Defending the wisdom of your years over your knowledge of *things*

If you circled mostly everything in Section One you may have exaggerated a bit. Take a closer look again in the mirror and you'll see you don't look so bad. If you circled mostly everything in Section Two you may have overreacted. Get a tissue, stop crying, and continue reading. If you circled mostly everything in Section Three you may be underestimating yourself. Don't worry about a thing—you probably won't remember your score tomorrow.

Have you been around a young kid lately? How do they see the world? In short: filled with infinite possibilities. Children see few limits to the possibilities life has waiting for them. Your own child may have wanted to be an astronaut, the president, or a fireman—and something else entirely the next week. They'll change their mind tomorrow, or the next day, or whenever they find something more appealing—which, by the way, is exactly how you felt at that age. (Trust me, if you can't remember.) Kids' innocence and pure joy with the world are amusing to us, but, honestly, when was the last time you felt this way *about anything?* We can laugh at them—and wish that we were able to have that same sense of amazement with the world—at the same time.

Likewise, what's so tough about being old? What's so depressing about it? In a word: restrictions. You've probably heard someone close to you say: *I'm too old. I can't do that anymore. I'm too old to start a new career, too tired to enjoy playing like I used to, too worried that I'll fall and get hurt.* Sure, when you catch yourself talking like that, you might realize that what you're saying is entirely practical, logical, and completely understandable. But that doesn't mean it isn't downright depressing.

I truly believe that middle age is more than any ill-defined, vague twenty or thirty-year age range, or a laundry list of physical changes, or some shifts in our personal relationships, work patterns. *Instead, I believe that middle age represents an attitudinal shift from seeing our life as filled with possibilities to seeing it as made up of restrictions.*

When we are young, everything is possible; when we are old, everything seems to have restrictions. Middle age, then, becomes that point where we begin seeing our life as restrictions and not possibilities. Sure, it's a matter of perspective and "all we have to do" is change our perspective. Some of us make that shift overnight—the fifty-year-old with a brand new, bright red sports car comes to mind. Others change gradually, letting it pile it on, and sometimes barely even notice the gradual changes until they look in the mirror and are staring at a stranger.

It doesn't have to be that way.

Yes, it is possible to focus on midlife as a period of gain. Wisdom, freedom from putting the needs of others first, independence, new social networks, and great strength and capacity are all possibilities. Midlife need not mean the end of the line, retreat into the sunset, or being tossed to the side of the road. Instead, middle age can be an opportunity for reinvention in unprecedented ways.

Whether or not midlife means a whole new script, it is a time when we can shape our lives without all of the "should or shouldn't haves" that may have constrained us earlier. It will take some work and effort on your part, but you have all the tools at your disposal, right now. Midlife does not have to be all "restrictions"—unless we let it be. You have already taken the first big step by acknowledging that you want to change. *Before you know it—with the help of this book—you will be seeing more of the possibilities in life!*

2

YOU'RE SO VAIN

The Physical Changes

of Middle Age

BACKGROUND

IT CAN BE as subtle as your dearest friend (or child) reaching over the table to yank a gray hair out of your head—probably as you are struggling at the same time to read the small print on the menu. And while no one would think to remove a silver lock from your husband's hair (that's right, silver; he's not turning gray after all, he's becoming "distinguished") he most likely is, at least privately, noticing his receding hairline, or a few new gray chest hairs. You and your mate may go about your daily lives pretending to be young (or at least choosing to deny that you are getting older). In reality, you find yourself more often than not in bed by ten and really wanting to go to sleep—as opposed to the times when going to bed meant something entirely different. And while you may or may not remember exactly where you were when you first noticed the signs of middle age, you are definitely noticing them now.

How we age is affected by a variety of things: our heredity, our diet, health, education, and a whole lot more. Take a good look at your parents. How well did they age? What did they feed you growing up? Factors such as the cultural heritage, educational level, and economic status of your parents have a tremendous effect on your diet and nutritional habits today. If pizza, fries, and other fast food constituted a healthy meal in your house, or if pasta and bread were an every meal staple, then chances are you may have never learned to eat right, and as a result are struggling to lose those few extra pounds or struggling to keep your cholesterol down. After all, it is not so easy to learn to love tofu after a lifetime of eating tortellini. Even factors such as where you grew up can affect how you age. Okay, so at one time you were proud to be a California *Baywatch* babe or Florida's number one water-ski champion; but you may be paying the price now as your skin is looking a little sun damaged. Consider yourself lucky at the class reunion when you run into an aging classmate who by the looks of their sagging skin, frail posture, and dentures looks like they should have graduated with your older brother. The point here is that where you are today physically didn't just happen overnight—and it's not all your fault.

Let's get the bad news out of the way first: the truth is, each of our five senses do tend to change as we progress through middle age. But don't get alarmed. These changes are gradual. Hearing is typically the first to change, beginning in our mid-40s. In our mid-50s, our vision and sense of touch tend to decline slightly, followed by taste later in that decade. Smell is typically the last to begin any significant change, usually holding off until the mid-70s in the average healthy person.

However, there is good news. Age-related changes differ greatly from one person to the next—just as we experience developmental changes differently in our infancy, childhood, and teens. One person may encounter vision problems, with no changes in hearing; another may go well into his later years with no noticeable changes in the five senses. This is a good time to look how your parents and relatives have aged, by the way. It's your chance to prove, or disprove, the "apple doesn't fall far from the tree" theory. Chances are you may be lucky enough to have your mother's youthful skin, or grandfather's full head of hair. However, if you're not so fortunate and are beginning to notice some male pattern baldness—go ahead and blame your mother. *(Hey we blame mothers for everything else that goes wrong in a child's life—so why not this?)*

Because we each cope and react differently, *the effect* of aging differs among individuals. For those whose identity is not tied directly to the appearance a few pounds and a wrinkle here and there, this is no big deal. But, for women at middle age who are struggling with the fact that they are no longer young, having to wear bifocals to see the small print, or having to wear support pantyhose to make sure no one else sees the varicose veins can be devastating. How you feel about yourself, and what you have been taught about aging also affects how you react. In some cultures aging brings respect and position, but in America it too often brings layoffs, and loneliness.

Also, how you age depends in a large part of how you prepare to age. What you do at twenty or thirty has a tremendous effect on your midlife health. Do not be shocked when, at age sixty, you can't jog a mile around the neighborhood—when you haven't walked it—ever. Remember those hours of tanning on the beach, those all-day tennis matches, or hours of yard work without sunscreen? They're here now, in all those wrinkles on your forehead, or discoloration in your hands, or aching muscles.

There's another myth about aging that needs to be addressed, too. There are no sharp differences that occur either physically or psychologically the day a person turns sixty-five. No clinical evidence exists for selecting this chronological age as a retirement age. Some impairments and deficiencies do occur as a person ages, but we often find ways of adjusting, compensating or maladjusting, which are discussed later on in this chapter.

The most important thing to remember is that aging is not a disease. Whatever changes come with aging, most people in their midlife years are in relatively good health. Physiological, sensory, emotional, and physical changes do occur, but the human body and a person's subtle—and often unnoticed and quite ingenious—methods of compensation often allow them to successfully function in today's complex world.

SYMPTOMS

THE SIGNS AND symptoms of aging include physical, emotional, social, and cognitive changes. The physical changes tend to drive most of our feelings, thoughts, and behaviors. Following are some of the common symptoms our changing bodies bring with us into middle age that everyone seems to notice (and complain about), and other, less common ones, that may point to more serious problems.

Common symptoms: (Sorry, no matter how many times a week you go to the gym, or how many times a month you dye those silver roots, these symptoms catch up with even the best of us):

- Hair loss
- Thinning hair
- Graying hair
- Weight gain
- Clothes that don't seem to fit as well
- Weight "shift"—you weigh the same, but the pounds have transferred to different parts of your body
- Loss of strength
- Less energy overall
- More frequent colds, illness, etc.
- Memory loss
- Decreased sexual desire
- Performance anxiety (more common in men)
- Hot sweats (for women)
- Moodiness (men *and* women—sorry guys, this one is an equal opportunity symptom)

Serious Symptoms: Note that these warrant a call to your doctor if you, or someone you love and trust, have noticed changes in your eating habits (often driven by wanting that youthful figure back or wanting that not so youthful husband back):

- **Signs of anorexia:** loss of a significant amount of weight; continuing to diet although you are already thin; feeling fat even after losing weight; an intense fear of weight gain; preoccupation with food; preferring to diet in isolation; cooking for others and not yourself; excessive or sudden hair loss; exercising compulsively; lying about eating; depression; anxiety; hyperactivity.
- **Signs of bulimia:** bingeing or eating uncontrollably; purging by strict dieting; fasting; unhealthy levels of vigorous exercise; vomiting or abusing laxatives or diuretics in an attempt to lose weight; using the bathroom frequently after meals; preoccupation with

body weight; depression; mood swings; feeling out of control; vomiting blood; and bloodshot eyes.

- **Signs of binge eating:** episodes of binge eating; eating when not actually hungry; frequent dieting; feeling unable to stop eating voluntarily; awareness that eating patterns are abnormal; weight fluctuations; depressed mood; feeling ashamed about your eating behaviors; antisocial behavior; and obesity.

PRESENTING PROBLEMS

The Real Skinny on Weight Gain

As we are too often reminded by our doctors, and by every magazine that we pick up from a shelf, an extra 100 calories or so a day can cause a ten-pound weight gain over the course of a year. (Do the math: that extra slice of pizza can really do some long-term damage.) Sure, we know that those extra calories can be burned up by a brisk twenty or thirty-minute daily walk—but, of course, those walks are also very easy to put off.

If you've been putting off those daily walks, and watching the weight creep up on you, you are definitely not alone.

Sure, we are all lazy from time to time, and many of us need to get more serious about our health, but there are four growing trends that are common with boomers today that help explain this shift that occurs in midlife: **changes in body chemistry, a decrease in activities, changing lifestyle patters, and unfulfilled lives.** Okay, we notice (and so does everyone else) that we are slowing down as we age—but that is not such a bad thing. Let's look a little further at each of these.

Changes in Body Chemistry: Studies illustrate that beginning at about age thirty we begin to lose a small percentage of muscle mass every decade. While this may be a great excuse to have someone else take the groceries from the car, the bad news is that our metabolism (the speed with which our body breaks down the food we eat) also begins gradually to slow down. (Maybe our kids are right when they say that we are driving too slowly, not thinking fast enough.) But this loss of muscle mass and decrease in metabolism working together lead to one very odd peculiarity: Our clothes start getting tighter, while the scale reads the same because the muscle we are losing "makes up" for the fat we gain. (What a wonderful tradeoff, right?) We lose important muscle, and start gaining more fat around our middle, legs, and bottoms.

A Decrease in Activities: As our nests empty, our lives become less active. There are no more kids to chase after, or teens to drive around. We seem to sit around and watch more TV (wasn't that something you used to yell at your kids about?). The abundance of cooking shows available only increases our appetites. Perhaps an old injury or a new ailment prevents us from doing things. Or our better jobs demand that we travel more, reach for more fast food, spend more time sitting on airplanes, and pecking away at our laptops. For many of us, now that we are older and more successful, our more demanding jobs rule out getting to the gym, taking time for physical work around the house, or spending the extra time required to cook a homemade meal as much as we would like. Technology doesn't help, either. We no longer have to walk upstairs or to the boss's office to deliver a message. We can just text them, send an e-mail, or call on our cell.

Changing Lifestyle Patterns: As baby boomers move into their later forties and fifties, and now their sixties, we are confronted with new increasing challenges at keeping our weight in check. As new or soon to be "empty nesters" without our little ones at home, there is less motivation to cook balanced meals ("why bother, it's just the two of us," or if it's "just" me eating) and we tend to eat out more, or just "throw together" something quick and easy. Unfortunately, this leads us to eat less healthfully and downplay weight control.

Unfulfilled Lives: Plain old overeating causes weight gain—and many times overeating is about more than just nourishment. As we hit middle age, overeating is usually not about that chocolate cake you crave, or the bowl of pasta you can't resist, it is about emotions.

Overeating can provide you both the comfort and control to "fill" some empty void. If you find yourself eating too much, take a look at your life: there is probably some aspect of your life—whether it's family, career, finances, whatever—that is left unfulfilled. The reality is that no amount of ice cream, or brownies, or popcorn, can fill the void.

Weigh the Benefits of Constant Dieting

Many of us decide to diet our way through midlife—vowing that we'll splurge in our older years. We expect that tomorrow will be better if we are just a little thinner, and our burdens will become a little lighter. Midlife can be tough, and obsessing over fat content and caloric intake can take your mind off your ex-husband, or your aging parents for a few weeks. But most likely you are still no happier than you were before you took that bite of your sugar-free, low-cal, whole wheat, oatmeal raisin muffin.

Somehow we think that we have *permission* to be fatter and less fit when we enter our seventies, but I have heard (from my own mother . . . a hundred times) that the doctors will argue with us about taking that extra weight off more than they do now. So, dieting and eating healthy is something that does not end at midlife (sadly, for all of us). Constant dieting can be an excuse to avoid the issues that are really bothering you. It makes little sense to look so great on the outside, when you feel so miserable on the inside. **When you are preoccupied with dieting and looking great sometimes what you reveal to the outside is just not so pretty. Dieting can cause irritability, depression, and fatigue. Your obsession with food or caloric intake can become obsessive and obvious to those around you (not to mention annoying).** Getting a new mind-set toward eating and changing your life does make sense.

Dieting makes the mind hungry and often results in:

- Preoccupation with food
- Binge eating
- Irritability

- Depression
- Fatigue
- Social withdrawal
- Poor concentration

IDENTIFY THE PATTERNS THAT CONTINUALLY TRIP UP YOUR WEIGHT LOSS

Take a look at what and when you eat, particularly the "wrong foods." More importantly, try to discern exactly *why* you are turning to food at these times. Understanding the reasons you eat when you are not hungry or why you crave those indulgent "comfort" foods can be a powerful tool.

- **Log your binge or "bad food" eating for a day or two** by identifying the events that occur right before you rush to the fridge or pizzeria. Take the time to jot these down on paper. (For example, "Had an argument with mom about finances," "Fought about how we're raising our son.")
- **After a week, examine your list of what caused the binges to see if there are any patterns.** You will most likely discover that for many of the events on your list, there is some underlying issue that continually sets off your need to eat. For example, you may get a call from your son or daughter telling you that they can't make it home from college this weekend to help you shop for dad's fiftieth surprise birthday party because there is a big football game at school. The real problem is not that you won't have anyone to help you shop (you've thrown enough parties by this time in your life and I am sure that you can do a fine job by yourself), but that you are afraid of losing control of your child. Everything and anything that remotely contributes to the realization that *your child is growing up and becoming independent* is the real issue.

- **Take some time to address the root cause, not the actual event.** Why are you feeling like this? Why, exactly, are you so threatened by the thought of your child growing up? Take some time to talk with your child about how you feel. Schedule some time to make up for that lost weekend shopping together—and just as importantly, schedule some activities for yourself.

Poor Body Image, Poor Self-Esteem

No one is more critical about the way you look than yourself. As teens we develop what is called an imaginary audience. This is a group of people who exist only in our minds, who judge and criticize what we wear, who we are, and what we look like. Some adults however, are unable to grow up and step off the stage and leave the audience behind, and as a result they never are able to see their own beauty. Body image is our internal picture of our outer self, including how we see, think, and feel about our body. The body image that we have today derives, in large part, from our lifetime experiences—including whether we have always been admired for our physical appearance, or if we have had a weight problem and have been teased about it. The people that we love most—our parents, grandparents, and siblings—and even those we detested like school bullies and the teenage beauty queen—are in some way responsible for shaping how we feel about our bodies today. Women and men well into their sixties still recall the trauma and confusion that surrounded puberty, as they got a preview of the new adult body they would soon grow to love or hate.

Today, our celebrity-obsessed society has never been more focused—for both the young and old among us—on physical appearance as a prerequisite for success and belongingness. While this affects both men and women, it strikes women particularly hard, as they already face various challenges due to biological changes, and a culture providing few healthy, strong images of older women. Women who don't have a strong, healthy self-image, tend to believe the mass media message that taking control over one's body by dieting, exercising, or even plastic surgery will help them take control over their lives. (No one tells them that no matter how good they look they can't control their boss or their children.) Problems occur when women begin to believe that looking good is the solution to gaining control.

It helps to have a good body image in our culture because it often is closely linked to self-esteem, ("I look good therefore I am a good person.") Our body image can even affect our ability to make healthy lifestyle choices, such as whether to exercise or not. Physician and psychologist William Sheldon bridged the connection between body types and personality by identifying how each of several different body types is characteristic of certain personalities. Sheldon assigned people into three categories of body types: endomorphic, mesomorphic, and ectomorphic.

IS YOUR BODY TYPE AFFECTING HOW YOU SEE YOURSELF?

Does your personality change along with the numbers on the scale, or with your? Are you shy because you are self-conscious about being too tall and skinny? Are you comfortable around food, around people, and about being "a little round?" Do you feel confident only when you feel fit and in good shape?

According to Dr. Sheldon's Theory:

- **Endomorphs** have fat, soft, and round body types; their personality is described as relaxed, and sociable.
- **Mesomorphs** are muscular, rectangular, strong, and are filled with energy, and they have assertive personality tendencies.
- **Ectomorphs** are thin, long, fragile, artistic, and introverted; they tend to think about life, rather than consuming it or acting on it.

Today, women of all ages seem to find a way to attribute their success and failure in life to their attractiveness. Some will proudly tell you that the best job they ever had (or the best husband they ever had) was when they weighed 105 pounds and wore a size 4. (Yes, today size 4 is the new size 8. Scary, I agree.) Although they don't like to admit it, some women will say that their loneliest days and toughest times were when they had no money in their wallets for a haircut and color, no time away from the kids or the office for the gym.

Consider This

- 47% of healthy-weight women believe they are overweight.
- Less than a quarter of young women are satisfied with their bodies but by about 70 years of age, 50% of women are satisfied.
- There is evidence older women still diet regularly. In one study 30% of elderly women were on a diet, potentially putting them at risk of nutritional deficiency.

THE VICIOUS CYCLE OF POOR BODY IMAGE AND POOR HEALTH

It's no surprise that healthier people rate their body image better than those who are less healthy, and that people who exercise regularly have a better body image than those who don't. A person with high self-esteem is more self-accepting, possesses high self-worth, and has a positive self-image, while a person with low self-esteem is often self-critical, has low self-worth, and has a negative self-image. Poor body image can stop people from beginning regular physical activity (suddenly a CEO reverts to childhood fears that "they'll talk about how fat I look when they see me at the gym"), cause them to set unrealistic goals (I need to lose twenty pounds—this week!), and eventually push many to give up altogether. (And that's not to mention the pressure that comes along with being able to look good in those trendy exercise clothes.) Poor body image can also affect comfortableness with our sexuality and even everyday socializing. And there is strong evidence to support the fact that a poor body image is associated with mental health concerns like stress, anxiety, depression, and low self-esteem.

Take a Good Look at Yourself—and Appreciate Just Being You

Make a list of all the things you have been putting off for when you are thin; pick the one that you find the least threatening, and try it today. A good one to start with may be doing what I call a "Closet Cleansing." Look at all the clothes in your closet that you have not worn in months, maybe even in years. You know, the ones that you are saving until you get "thin." Stack them in "size order"—literally. Try to figure out how long it has been since you were the smallest size. If it was in high school, don't get upset: Get real. That was twenty or thirty years ago. Pack them up and move them out. When you finally reach a stack of clothes that fit a month ago, or a year ago, set a realistic date to fit in them. And DON'T buy yourself anything new until you do. Hard work has its reward. You will find a new you, looking great in your old clothes.

Eating Disorders: When Concern Turns to Obsession

In a society where, for many of us, thinness is equated with success and happiness, nearly every American woman, man, and child at one time or another has struggled with dieting, and ideas about weight and body shape. Body image distortion occurs more frequently for women than for men, and in some women, the obsession with being thin starts young and can last a lifetime. Even as adults—and even for adults who don't have a distorted body image—our body image can affect how we feel about ourselves, interact with others, tend to our appearance on a day-to-day basis, and even the actions we take to maintain that image. As we discussed earlier, there is more to body image than what we see in the mirror: It derives from a combination of how we feel about our overall looks and how we react emotionally in certain situations. For some, the pressure to be thin can actually lead to eating disorders.

Crash dieting, fasting for short or long periods of time, bingeing, and purging are all signs of eating disorders—at any age. The media attention on the eating disorders of teenage girls makes us believe that eating disorders are something that women "grow out of" or never develop. That's not true. More and more women, in their 30s, 40s, and 50s and beyond suffer with disorders such as anorexia, bulimia, and binge eating. While some of these women first develop their eating disorders as adults, most have secretly struggled with an eating disorder their entire lives (and haven't sought treatment), or were treated for eating disorders when they were younger and have developed a recurrence in middle age. Women often develop eating disorders because they look to an area where they can have self-discipline or achieve perfection to compensate for difficult changes and challenges they may be facing.

Although women are generally associated with eating disorders, men of all ages can—and do—have eating disorders. Adult men with eating disorders typically have a history of being overweight or obese and may be striving for a more athletic or muscular build. Although men less often turn to vomiting as a way to purge, they typically turn to compulsive exercise, and weight-loss or weight-gain supplements. Eating disorders have dangerous health effects at any age. (Older women are especially at risk because other health conditions may make them especially vulnerable to the effects of eating disorders.)

Take a Look at Yourself and Tell the Truth

Stand in front of a mirror naked and say out loud the things about your body you don't like. (This part seems to be easy for most women because we are so critical of our bodies.) The words sagging breasts, varicose veins, and jelly belly might come to mind. Now, the hard part is finding and saying out loud those things that you still find are beautiful about you. (To help you prepare for this exercise keep a log of the common compliments you receive.) Promise yourself that you will continue to take notice and not forget that beauty is in the eye of the beholder—that's you.

The Most Common Eating Disorders and Their Root Causes

- **Anorexia** is an intense fear of fat, and a preoccupation with food and weight that often hides other underlying psychological problems. Anorexics may not admit that their weight loss or restrictive eating is a problem.
- **Bulimia nervosa** is a disorder in which frequent episodes of binge eating are followed by purging (ridding the body of food), and can involve vomiting, abusing laxatives and/or diuretics, exercising compulsively, or fasting. Bingeing and purging are often followed by intense feelings of guilt and shame. Like anorexics, bulimics use self-destructive eating behaviors to deal with much deeper psychological problems. Bulimics often feel out of control and recognize that their behavior is not normal.
- **Binge eating disorder** or compulsive overeating, involves uncontrolled eating that is usually kept a secret. People with this condition engage in frequent binges, but unlike bulimics, do not purge afterward. Like bulimics, though, binges are usually followed by intense feelings of guilt and shame. Here, too, food is used as a dysfunctional coping mechanism; people with binge eating disorders often have depression or other psychological problems.

Am I out of my mind to be so concerned with my body? If you feel that you may be suffering from an eating disorder, consider the three most common causes, below, and seek professional help:

- **A Fear of Aging:** The term "American Beauty" traditionally does not describe a middle age women in her prime of life. Although women in their 40s, 50s, and 60s have gained years of wisdom, their value as important and respected members of society lessens. As their youthful looks start to change, their value begins to decline. Women often begin compulsive dieting and excessive exercising after midlife divorces thinking that in order to attract new partners they must develop bodies like their twenty-five-year-old competition. Don't be fooled: Although men during this time don't become as obsessed over their bodies they do try hard to create a "younger" look for themselves.

■ **Personal demands**: Work, children, spouses, personal lives, and (increasingly) aging parents often accumulate quickly and make even the most put-together woman feel she is losing control. In a desperate search for something she can control many women begin focusing on food, weight, and appearance to distract them from thinking about the other stresses they live with. (Not consciously, of course, but something drives you to eat the entire bag of cookies before bed, or to wake up at 5:00 AM so you will have time for a two hour workout before your forty-five minute power walk to work.) You may think food and exercise can satisfy that "need" for control, that this behavior is a reward for all you have to "put up with" lately, but in the long term it will create one more problem for you.

■ **Greater awareness of diet, weight, and health**: Many illnesses are related to what we eat and weigh. As we age, we become more aware of the impact of our eating decisions. And even if we want to hide from the facts our doctors, our newscasters, and neighbors always seem to remind us. Women and men feel obligated and pressured to stay healthy (that is a good thing), but often cannot develop healthy eating habits without getting obsessed about them. Becoming overly preoccupied about your weight and appearance is not all that good for your physical and emotional health.

Get Comfortable in Your Skin

Act like a person comfortable with her body: watch what happens to the way you walk, interact with others, or eat. Notice how different you act and feel on a "good hair" or "good outfit" day. Try to imagine how good you would feel having all "good body" days. Practice feeling good in your own body. Go somewhere where you don't really know anyone (do some errands at a mall on the other side of town, drive to a different grocery store on your way home, or have the bus let you off on a different stop). Change your posture, stand up straight and imagine that everyone is noting how good you look. Notice how people react to your new confidence and new attitude. You will see the difference. Once you get used to doing this and feeling comfortable, it will be easy to do this around the people you know, or the people you want to know better.

DON'T FORGET WHAT MAKES YOU SPECIAL IN THE FIRST PLACE

Think back on what it was that made you feel good about yourself in your younger years: was it your great sense of humor, or your off-beat sense of style? Chances are, those qualities are still as appealing as ever—and perhaps more so. By shifting your focus to your attributes—and away from your perceived flaws—you can boost your self-esteem and reestablish your own standards for attractiveness.

Foster an Attitude of Body Acceptance

It's funny how much we will obsess over, say, our nose or hips, but then how quickly we forget that it takes our *whole body and mind*—and not just the parts we stress over—to enjoy our lives.

- Don't compare yourself to the unrealistic, stereotypical, superficial standards that are celebrated by our media (or your best friend's sister).
- Don't spend too much money on products to change "skin-deep" factors like wrinkles. But do spend money on the things that make you feel good. There are no miracle creams. Much of aging is genetic and there is only so much you (or your plastic surgeon) can do.
- Do focus on how your whole body, rather than the "parts" that you don't like as much. Come on, nothing in life is all bad.

- Don't go shopping for clothes when you are feeling vulnerable or when you feel bloated or fat (or are having a bad hair day).
- Don't shop in stores that are just not your style—in general, buy clothes that you feel good in and that fit you well. Dress your age. There is reason that older women who dress well are called "smartly dressed." With age come all kinds of wisdom. Make sure that being happy does not depend on avoiding wrinkles, gray hair or body fat. Look for inner beauty. It doesn't cost as much to maintain.

Cognitive Decline:
We're Not as Sharp as We Once Were

Sigmund Freud, at age 51 said:

> *"About the age of 50, the elasticity of the mental processes on which treatment depends is, as a rule, lacking. Old people are no longer educable."*

. . . and went on to do much of his best work in his 50s and 60s.

The above quote is also proof that even the best of us tend to focus on the negative parts of aging. In fact, even many experts often define "successful" aging as the effective management of decay and decline. (Pretty bleak stuff, correct?) However, this line of thinking is already out of date: no one can deny that aging brings challenges and losses, but recent discoveries in neuroscience show that our aging brain is more flexible and adaptable than we previously thought.

New studies suggest that the brain's left and right hemispheres become better integrated during middle age, which makes way for greater creativity. Age also seems to dampen some negative emotions. In addition, research has confirmed that the old "use it or lose it" adage applies here, and that the aging brain grows stronger from use and challenge. In short, midlife is a time of new possibility. Growing old can be filled with positive experiences. Ready for more good news?

Consider This

- Middle-aged people score higher on almost every measure of cognitive functioning than they did when they were twenty-five: verbal and numerical ability, reasoning and verbal memory all improve by midlife.
- The only ability that declines between twenty-five and midlife is perceptual speed: the ability to quickly and accurately perform tasks like deciding whether two zip codes are identical. (You've always lived by slow and steady wins the race, right?)

Remember: Even with a small decline in speed,

our mental abilities are well above what

they were in young adulthood.

Seek Support from Your Friends

If you find that you are depressed or discouraged by the aging process, stop complaining to friends that are just as depressed as you. Yes, misery loves company, but you will find yourself feeling a lot better talking to an older friend or relative that has been through the process and who can be an "older" role model, or the voice of experience. Look through a family album, and find that person whose look you like. Ask them about their secrets to aging. Remember: You share the same genes so maybe if things worked for them, they will work for you.

If you were to examine the brain of the average fifty-year-old with a high-powered microscope, you would find that it looks like a bunch of computer and cable wires tightly wired together. You don't have to be able to remember back to your college biology class to get what I'm saying here. One crucial difference between older and younger brains is easy to overlook: Older brains have learned more. (How many times do we remind our children, and twenty-five-year-old coworkers of this fact?) The density in your older brain reflects both deeper knowledge and superior judgment than that of your younger friends. If you doubt this, think about how age is generally regarded as such an advantage in fields like law, medicine, coaching, and management. There is no substitute for acquired learning. (So then, "older and wiser" really isn't an old wives' tale.)

Knowledge and wisdom are not the only fruits of age. Younger adults tend to use either their rational (left side of the brain) or intuitive (right side). Older adults, however, typically use both hemispheres when considering difficult decisions. Also, the area of the brain that controls our "fight or flight" response is known to mellow with age. Not surprisingly, then, older adults show less evidence of fear, anger, and hatred than younger adults. Psychological studies confirm this, proving that older adults are less impulsive and less likely to dwell on their negative feelings. Without revisiting that college biology class too much, suffice it to say that our brains actually improve with age.

So, the aging brain is more resilient, adaptable, and capable than we probably thought. However, that doesn't mean we should get lazy and coast on our newfound brainpower. There are several types of activity that can, if practiced regularly, help boost the power, clarity, and subtlety of your mind.

MENTAL STIMULATION: TAKE STEPS TO DELAY THE EFFECTS OF AGING

You know the benefits of regular physical exercise, and mental exercise is no different: There are real advantages to working out your mental muscles every day.

Whenever you learn something new, the nerve cells in your brain grow and the connections between those cells strengthen. Any activity that makes you concentrate will help exercise the mind and keep it strong. Particularly for those of us over forty, this is an invaluable source of improvement.

- Study a foreign language, sign up for a continuing education course. Do crossword puzzles if you're not already.
- Take up art or music lessons or start a new hobby that you always wanted to pursue, but pushed aside for "more important" things. We always made time for the kids to go to karate or guitar lessons. This should be the time of your life to learn something new. These kinds of activities help strengthen the part of the brain that controls spatial relations.
- Sharpen your hand-eye coordination and reaction time reflex by taking up a sport; playing a musical instrument, or even video games on the computer. This is your chance to justify buying the newest digital technology.
- Learn something new from a book or magazine, and try to enhance your memory by recalling that new information several times during each day. Try to explain or teach someone else about what you learned.
- Regular reading of the newspaper (better yet, a few newspapers or really challenge yourself with a foreign newspaper) will help, as will keeping your mind sharp by playing games like chess, cards, or Scrabble.
- Brushing your teeth with your nondominant hand, which activates little-used connections on the nondominant side of your brain. You can get creative here, too: try putting your shoes and socks on with your eyes closed. Breaking your daily routine in a challenging way will cause your brain to actively seek out new pathways to solutions. The use it or lose it theory does apply here.

INSIGHTS

FOR MOST PEOPLE, midlife arrives with a bit of a surprise. Despite what the calendar says, they do not feel older. However, they may somewhat reluctantly admit that they are no longer "youthful" and that they may have even lost some energy.

It is normal to be thinking about (and questioning) body changes and self-identity during midlife. However, what these physical body changes "mean" within our culture and to you personally may be a problem. A lot of how we feel, as individuals, about our bodies is taught to us from our culture and from our parents. While some societies respect women more for age, maturity, and wisdom, most western women feel that youthfulness and thinness are attractive and desirable and there is very little that is attractive about becoming older. Much damage is done by disordered eating and obsessive exercise—including diminished physical and mental health and impaired family, social, and professional lives. We seem to pay the price, and are still disappointed that our lives have not changed in ways we had hoped.

In reality, women can be fit, vital and attractive (or not so fit, vital and attractive) at any age. Increasing age in itself is not a license to become larger and more unfit. All women are different, but it is usual to gain some weight, change shape, lose skin elasticity, and for hair to turn gray or thin. When and how much these things happen varies—and depends upon—individual genetic tendencies and other factors that are out of our control. How you perceive these changes is in your control.

Many of us spend a lot of time trying to change our bodies due to self-confidence issues or lack of happiness rather than getting on with life. We do need to be realistic and sensible about whether we have a health issue related to being overweight, so that we can choose to make changes that would improve our health. You need to begin making these changes *now* and make them long term. Each woman needs to evaluate her own risk of age-related health problems such as osteoporosis, heart disease or diabetes, or weight-related joint problems, and work on lifestyle changes that can realistically help to prevent or manage these conditions. Prevention is the key here. I am not by any means saying that you can actually stop any of these things from happening, but you can at least try to reduce your risks.

In writing this book, I realized that our view of human development during midlife is very outdated. We tend to think of aging in purely negative terms, and even experts often define "successful" aging as the effective management of decay and decline. Nonsense. No one can deny that aging brings challenges and losses, but as we explored earlier in this chapter, science has shown that our aging brains are more flexible and adaptable than we ever thought. (And our bodies can be too if we exercise those muscles.) Age also seems to dampen many negative emotions, and the old "use it or lose it" adage is true: The aging brain actually grows stronger from use and challenge. In short, midlife is a time of new possibility. Growing old can be filled with positive experiences. The challenge is to recognize our potential—and nurture it.

DON'T SWEAT IT

Hormones, Menopause,
and the Viagra Revolution

BACKGROUND

PERHAPS YOUR MOTHER gave you the warning. Or maybe you overheard your father make jokes about the manic woman who keeps him up all night by turning the air up—and the covers down—all while she's complaining about how she is sweating. Meanwhile, your "older" menopausal girlfriends have most likely mentioned their lowered sex drive (not to mention their husband's, or boyfriend's, overzealous desire for Viagra). You probably paid all of this minimal attention (sorry, guys) until you wake up one night sweating—and suddenly "get it." You check the thermostat, check your own temperature, (perhaps even double-check your driver's license for your correct age), before realizing that everything is "normal." You are fifty, or perhaps even forty-five or fifty, and having your first hot flash.

It seemed like just yesterday that home pregnancy tests, colicky babies, and stretch marks were common terms in your vocabulary. Now it's varicose veins and Viagra? I know that we all think those ten extra pounds and one gray hair appeared overnight, but they didn't. And although a hot flash occurs suddenly, menopause is a process—and like all other processes—is different for every woman.

Likewise, so is the way we handle them. Many women suddenly feel like teenage girls again, afraid of the "changes," confused about what comes next, and—as the female hormones estrogen and progestin drop—feel as if puberty is starting all over. Still others are relieved that they are entering a more "mature" stage in life. And for some menopausal women who begin experiencing the slacking off of a monthly period, they all of a sudden become emotional at the idea that they will someday never need to buy a tampon again—a sign that her youth and childbearing years are about to come to an end. (Not a good time to remind her that she has been praying for this moment, off and on, for much of the last thirty years.)

Technically, you don't actually "hit" menopause until one year after your final menstrual period (don't forget to mark the date, so you don't miss your chance to celebrate). For American women, this happens at about age fifty-one, on average. The signs and symptoms of menopause, however, often appear long before this one-year anniversary when your ovaries shut down and you have no more periods. The process actually takes place over years and is commonly divided into two stages:

Perimenopause: The time when you begin experiencing menopausal signs and symptoms, even though you are still menstruating. Your hormone levels fluctuate unevenly, and you may have hot flashes and/or other symptoms; perimenopause may last four to five years or longer.

Postmenopause: Once twelve months have passed since your last period, you have reached menopause. Your ovaries produce much less estrogen, no progesterone, and release no eggs. The years that follow are called postmenopause.

Gone in a Hot Flash: The Realities of Menopause

The hormonal changes that come with menopause mean considerable changes for you. There will be decisions for you and your doctor to make regarding osteoporosis (a weakening of the bones as estrogen decreases). You'll weigh the benefits and risks of taking hormone replacement therapy (which your physician will surely discuss with you), and you'll think about how to keep off those extra few pounds.

And as if dealing with all these physical changes is not enough, there are considerable emotional issues to deal with, as well. Somehow, between those feelings of *being fat* and of *getting old*, you may find that hormonal changes cause you to have less patience for the generally passive female roles and duties you may once have performed (attending to everyone's needs before your own, performing household duties and the like). It seems—and your loved ones may be quick to remind you—that you easily express anger or frustration at everything and everyone. You may find yourself less tolerant of people-pleasing and domination by bosses or husbands, who have no idea what it is like to face the fact your childbearing years are ending. (Actually, now that you're thinking about it, they didn't understand it when you were complaining during pregnancy, either.)

It can all sound so depressing: the shutting down of ovaries and the "end of your childbearing years." But it is certainly not the end of your life. There are really many positive sides to menopause—no more cramps, no more pre-period or post-period stress, no more unsafe days, no more fear of unplanned or unwanted pregnancy, and no more worries about birth control. Menopause has its advantages once you get past the physical aspects and get a grip on the emotional issues. And understanding what these signs and symptoms are is the first step to dealing with them.

Symptoms: For Women Only

- Feelings of warmth deep within the chest that seem to flow upward and outward
- Increase in skin temperature, which can cause flushing of the neck and face
- Darkening red blotches on the chest, neck, and arms
- Sudden hot flashes that occur at night—and that are severe enough to wake you up—which are called night sweats and are sometimes followed by chills
- Difficulty sleeping or waking up for no apparent reason and being unable to get back to sleep. Fatigue and reduced energy throughout the day, irritability, anxiousness, nervousness, memory lapses, and difficulties concentrating

- Change in premenstrual symptoms. Missed periods, longer periods, and shorter periods.

Symptoms: For Men and Women

- Changes in skin tone
- Sagging skin from the loss of moisture and suppleness resulting in bags and wrinkles
- Damaged, dry, flaky "alligator" skin as a result of years of sun damage or smoking
- Spotted blotches on hands and face

Symptoms of a Reduced Libido: For Men and Women

- Feeling not "in the mood" more often
- Trouble achieving orgasm as regularly, or not at all
- Feeling "less sexual" overall or difficulty becoming aroused
- Less pleasurable sexual intercourse
- Feeling unattractive
- Depression, bereavement, stress, fatigue, performance anxiety, anger, and relationship problems

PRESENTING PROBLEMS

> *By the year 2010, there will be sixty million menopausal women in the United States.*
>
> *Wow, that is a lot of "hot" women OVER 40!*

If you are one of those millions, you may be finding that the declining estrogen levels associated with menopause can cause more than those annoying hot flashes. In fact, you may also be feeling that you are in a constant state of PMS (premenstrual syndrome). Unfortunately, emotional changes are a normal part of menopause, and women undergoing premenopause or menopause often report irritability, feelings of sadness, lack of motivation, anxiety, aggressiveness, difficulty concentrating, fatigue, mood changes, and tension. But these symptoms are not linked only to menopause. There are a number of conditions that can cause you to feel downright irritable—always make sure, with the help of your doctor, that a more serious condition is not causing you to feel this way.

During menopause, hormonal changes in our bodies create challenging feelings which, if ignored, remain below the surface and actually cause illness and make us feel worse about getting older.

Menopause actually resembles our passage through puberty (which I'm sure that you remember all too well). Adolescent girls often look in the mirror and see changes they don't like—or understand—and then become self-conscious. They may look at their peers and develop their own visions of what they should look like—and it's not always pretty. Does this sound familiar? Probably so. Middle-aged woman look at themselves and see a body they don't recognize. Not surprisingly, their husbands and families may be looking at them and seeing that their wife or mom is acting like someone they don't know!

There are many other psychological challenges that accompany this time, as well. Childbearing ends for most—but on the other end of the spectrum—many women today are having children later in life. These midlife moms face additional challenges, not the least of which is addressing the needs of young children while they themselves are facing hormonal and environmental changes.

COPING WITH THE EMOTIONAL CHANGES OF MENOPAUSE

Irritability and feelings of sadness are the most common emotional symptoms of menopause. However, they can often be managed through lifestyle changes, including learning ways to relax and reduce stress.

Everyone Needs a Healthy Outlet

- **Release your stress.** Exercise and eat healthy. Try kick-boxing and eat granola bars. I know you have heard that before, but it is just as important now as ever.

- **Find a calming pastime to practice**—like yoga, or meditation. To be time and cost efficient buy some CDs and do your stretching and relaxing at home, in the bathtub or during your lunch break at work. This way there is little or no excuse as to why you can't find the time.
- **Engage in a creative outlet that fosters a sense of achievement.** Go to pottery class, learn to knit (you can do that on the train or even while you are watching a movie). Plant something that you can nurture and watch grow. If you don't like orchids or daisies, how about an herb garden. (This might even spark your desire to cook more often.) Stay connected with your family and community. Entertain more. Throw a party to celebrate anything.
- **Nurture your friendships (walk, talk, listen, and laugh together).** Make new friends. Step out of the box a little and invite someone you have always wanted to be friends with to lunch.

Some women exhibit symptoms of depression during menopause, including boredom, exhaustion, self-questioning, irritability, unexpected anger, or acting on alcohol, drugs, food, or other compulsions. Greatly decreased or increased ambition, or feelings of worthlessness are other signs. (An important note: if your are feeling increasingly unable to cope, see your doctor. He or she may be able to recommend medication or some sort of individual or group therapy that can get you through this rough time.)

When women get older, our fear can intensify as we resist the idea of aging and death—as we fear becoming wrinkled and ugly, useless and neglected, or being helpless and poor or having no one to take care of us. It is tempting during these periods of vulnerability to cling to the past and not "let go," and get stuck. However, if we harden and resist, we will miss opportunities that might bring about change, transformation, and fulfillment. Perhaps worse, fear can also actually create disease through the stiffening, hardening, or constriction of our bodies. Stability is important, but too many women spend tremendous energy building security through buying and consuming "youth" products or having corrective surgery rather than listening to their inner callings.

Pack a Bag for a Blue Day

On those days that you feel a little down, are under a lot of stress, or feel somewhat lonely, pack a bag and just get out of the house (or office). Include a list of places that you want to go by yourself for thirty minutes, one hour, three hours, or eight hours. Find these in magazines, newspapers, or write them down if you hear about them some other way. Put some hidden cash and some day essentials for your last minute trip.

Keep the bag packed at all times—and when the moment strikes grab it and go!

DEAL WITH YOUR PHYSICAL, EMOTIONAL, AND SPIRITUAL HEALTH RIGHT NOW

You should plan for menopause now, even if you are not menopausal. Learn to eat right and minimize your stress now so when you're older, you won't have to unlearn a lot of bad habits. Be clear about what is important to you regarding your lifework, sexuality, marital status, childbearing, and fun. No matter where you are now, plan to be where you want to be and doing what you want to do with whom you want to do it—five years from now. Make plans—today—to be responsible, satisfied, and rewarded. Believe me, much of the stress of the golden years results from having to undo—or worse yet, pay the cost of—unwise youthful life choices.

Make a list of all the things that you need or want to change now in order to have a better second half of life. Use these three categories plus any of your own.

- **Health**—Eating and Exercise. Maybe no more double caffeine whipped cream lattes
- **Beauty and Skin Care**—Perhaps start buying makeup with sunscreen
- **Behavior and Bad Habits**—Try to stop calling your spouse all day at work
- **Attitude and Negative Thinking**—Stop telling yourself that you are old

Not in the Mood: Loss of Sex Drive

So, now at midlife we are free to create our own sexual revolution: There's no worry about getting pregnant, our sex partners can keep interested (or keep us interested) with the help of a tiny little pill. No one can say we're "too young" to be having sex (that's for sure). Sounds great—in theory. So what's the problem here? Women have spent their lives thus far "giving" (emotionally and physically) to everyone else first: rocking babies to sleep at 2:00 AM, comforting kids who didn't win the league championship, sewing Halloween costumes until our fingers fall off, and cooking meals that (mostly) everyone loved. Your sexual awakening will happen—as soon as you can catch up on your sleep.

But in all seriousness, there are other issues, too. For one, in our society, men are often seen as potential sex partners until an advanced age, but women are commonly considered to be over the hill (and decidedly not hot) by midlife. So many things are going on between you and your partner that issues like the diminished physical attractiveness of our partner, boring sexual routines, situational stress, marital problems, medical use of certain medications, and certainly the sudden drop in hormone levels, affect the midlife desire for sex. All of these issues may involve sexual desire or interest, arousal, orgasm, enjoyment, or frequency of sexual activity. So many different things change in every facet of women's lives during midlife that it becomes hard to identify what it is that we really need or want—and rarely is sex on the top of our priority list.

However, once your household gets quiet and you stop to look at what's ahead, a long look in the mirror will help shape that road. Body image has often had a big influence on sexual attitudes and activity throughout your life—and can affect sexual behavior in midlife even more. Sexual attractiveness, weight issues, and physical condition affect our sexuality.

Throughout women's lives, their weight tends to be a recurring issue, and this concern is quite evident among midlife women. Physiologically, the body's metabolic rate slows down with age and is accompanied by a decrease in lean body tissue and an increase in fat. This conflicts with the standards of attractiveness for women in American society. Youthfulness and a slender body? No wonder a middle-age woman has some anxiety about how her aging will affect her sexuality. The stereotypical image of older women is pretty much being "unattractive" and "asexual." Really: how many Victoria Secret's models have you ever seen over the age of forty? (Actually, get real: over the age of twenty-four?) With all the media marketing dollars behind Viagra you would think that the commercials would at least try to portray the wives of the over-fifty set as sexy—but they don't.

Midlife and after is also a time when profound lifestyle changes take place. Events like retirement and children leaving home can upset decades-long patterns in a couple's life. Many couples go through a period of adjustment when the kids move out or one or both of them retire. As a result the time a couple spends together alone increases. After years of being distracted by kids and ignoring one another's needs it can be difficult for midlife couples to connect at both an emotional and physical level. One bonus is that spending more time alone together gives you the time and freedom for real intimacy—something you may have lacked for many years (hello, decades?). One danger, however, is that couples who begin spending a lot of time together may stop making an effort to include romance in their relationship (of course, that doesn't describe you, right?).

The Brain is the Body's Most Important Sex Organ

Although working sex organs, adequate hormone levels, and certain minimal health levels are prerequisites for sexual activity—these elements do not necessarily guarantee sexual satisfaction. Other factors (combined with normal physical changes) can make anyone vulnerable to sexual problems especially during midlife. These include:

Stress and fatigue: During midlife, stress can hit from just about any direction—including challenging teenagers, financial worries, aging parents, health concerns (yours or a loved one's), and career problems are just a few. With so many demands on your time, attention, and sanity, a loving relationship may fall by the wayside, leading to a poor sexual connection. Stress has a particularly harsh effect on libido, especially in women. Whereas men can sometimes use sex to relax, women more often need to be relaxed in order to enjoy sex—a mismatch you may well be aware of.

Sheer lack of time: The physical changes that accompany aging (for both sexes) means that it may take you and your partner more time to become aroused and reach orgasm than it did in your younger years. You may find it difficult to make time for sex into an already packed day, or week. And many couples still remain in the old routine of waiting until bedtime to have sex (although with your crazy work hours who knows what time that would even be?). That might have worked well when you were younger and had to wait for the kids to go to sleep first—but at this point sheer exhaustion becomes an obstacle.

Expectations and past experiences: Your sexuality is a natural drive that's with you from your adolescence, but family, culture, and our religious background shape attitudes toward sex, as well. And as you become an adult, your own experiences further influence your sexuality. While many of us develop a healthy enjoyment of sex, others don't. Each individual needs to be comfortable with their own sexuality. What you have experienced in the past, or been taught in the past may not hold true today. This is the time in your life to lie back and clarify your own value system.

Chronic illness: Being sick or undergoing treatment for a condition may cause sexual difficulties that were never a problem before. Healthy partners can worry that sexual activity will worsen their loved one's condition. Sometimes not openly discussing this with your doctor and your partner can bring unnecessary worry and anxiety about sexual performance issues. Additionally, the fatigue and stress that comes with a caretaker role may also dampen the desire for sex.

Embarrassment discussing sexual matters often hinders people from fully expressing themselves sexually. Most likely this resistance or discomfort of talking about sex is something that began in childhood and is carried into adulthood. With the many emotional and physical changes that both men and women experience in midlife, changes in sexual relationships will also take place. Many men feel that their masculinity is challenged in the bedroom, and their self-worth hinges on good performance. As men get older and experience changes in their sexual performance it is not uncommon for them to have feelings of inadequacy that can interfere with a couple's intimate relationship.

At this turning point, some women feel that once they reach menopause their sexual "duties" are fulfilled and their sexual life is over. It is not uncommon for women to feel frumpy and sexually unattractive. And if her husband is still interested in sex (which he most likely is), a conflict is likely to erupt. Women who don't feel this way and who want to continue a healthy and active sex life must deal with their own performance anxieties in different ways. They may be worried that sex will be uncomfortable or worry that they are not, in fact, a "good lover."

Starting a new sexual relationship after a divorce or a spouse's death: People sometimes fear what sex will be like with a new partner. As much as someone may look forward to having a new sexual relationship, they also may be self-conscious about baring their body in front of someone new. Many midlife men and women don't like to look at themselves in the mirror when no one is looking, so you can understand the fear and anxiety of sharing that picture with anyone else for the first time! Another common worry when starting a new sexual relationship is performance. Because a new relationship may come along months or years after their last sexual relationship, some individuals feel anxious that "the equipment doesn't work anymore." And if it does, will they remember how to use it properly? (As was discussed earlier, memory really isn't on the decline so you should be okay here.)

Putting it Together: The Psychological/Sexual Connection

Sexual performance is not all in your mind. In order for people at any age to enjoy normal sexual functioning, physiological and biological factors have to be in good working order. When there are sexual performance problems, it is a good time to consider that psychological disorders could be the cause. These situations are so prevalent in our society that they have been given their own names: clinically known as Inhibited Sexual Desire (ISD) and hypoactive sexual desire disorder (HSDD). The most common cause of ISD seems to be difficulty in a personal relationship; specifically communication problems, lack of affection that is not associated with sexual intercourse, power struggles and conflicts, and a lack of time alone together. ISD may also be associated with a very restrictive upbringing concerning sex, negative attitudes toward sex, or negative or traumatic sexual experiences (such as incest, or sexual abuse).

According to the Diagnostic and Statistical Manual of Psychiatric Disorder IV a diagnosis of HSDD refers to a persistent or recurring lack of desire or an absence of sexual fantasies. However, sexual performance may be adequate once activity has been initiated. This disorder is more common in women, though it does affect both sexes if a partner does not feel emotionally intimate or close to their mate. I suggest that you consult with your physcian or a therapist who specializes in these disorders if you are concerned.

IMPROVE COMMUNICATION

Communication is essential for building the trust required for a successful sexual relationship. By talking frankly about your feelings, you and your partner can work on finding solutions to issues, and help prevent resentments from piling up. When conversation breaks down, anger and resentment are likely to build. But, one piece of advice: Don't have these intimate discussions while you are initiating sex. There is a time and place for everything, and usually talking about sexual problems during sex is not the most effective way to be heard. Wait for a quiet and comfortable intimate moment alone to have this discussion.

Dialogue is especially vital as physical changes take place. Let your partner know how you are physically feeling about some of your midlife changes. Talk about things that might help, or that you may require in order to have more pleasurable sex. No shame in asking because difficulties can be wrongly perceived as waning interest in sex, which can trigger feelings of rejection and resentment. By articulating feelings, you can sort out the physiological factors from the emotional and relationship issues, and address each appropriately.

Counteract Boredom

After decades of marriage, almost every couple has to contend with some sexual boredom sooner or later. The person who once captivated your soul and filled your heart with lust, years later barely holds your interest in the bedroom. Sex may not even seem worth the trouble or time when you're facing the same old lovemaking routines.

When sexual activity wanes, other types of physical affection often fade, too. This lack of physical connection often creates emotional distance between you and your partner. As a result, it's all the more difficult to resume sexual intimacy later on. But it is possible to do so—and you can even take your intimate relationship to new heights. Because inhibitions often lessen with age, sex at fifty or sixty can include a level of creativity and playfulness you would not have dreamed of in your younger years.

The following steps will help:

1. Do some warm-up exercises. S-l-o-w down: At your age, it takes longer to warm up (actually everything seems to take a little longer). Fortunately, one of the best things about midlife sex is that there is no urgency for our partners, and no curfew. Enjoy quality snuggle time before, during, and after sex

2. Don't kiss it goodbye. Kissing and holding help you bond with your partner, warm up, and enjoy the moment. Connect at a deep emotional level. Remember that "first" kiss? Make the atmosphere romantic.

3. Don't leave your sexy side at the party—bring it home with you. After a night, or an afternoon or morning, of looking great, and feeling sexy in that new outfit, or old tight jeans, don't rush to take them off when you come home. Stay with the feeling. Stay looking sexy. Your partner who might have admired you from across the room will be even more attracted when he admires you in his/her arms.

4. Do sexy things together long before it's time to hit the sheets: Make a date to have sex later. Leave reminder notes in each other's pockets. Skip the sweats and flannel pajamas. Wear something lace, play a romantic tune, and light some candles. Remember that your brain is the most important sexual organ so make the thought of making love stimulating.

5. Do wait for the right time to make love: Midnight sex after a romantic meal may have worked when we were young, but nowadays around 10 PM we're more likely to feel full, bloated, tired, and ready to sleep. Instead, set aside times that you know you will feel good and awake.

What's the Big Deal? The Viagra Revolution Is Giving Some Of Us a Headache

As the oldest baby boomers reach sixty, people are realizing that sex over sixty is possible and still exists for most couples. Women are assured that we can (and should) remain as sexually active as we were in our youth—just maybe a little more carefully so we don't hurt or break anything. If we are married, we are encouraged to spice up our sex lives. If we are single (and over 30 percent of females between 45 and 59 are), we are now free to initiate sexual adventures and seek new romantic partners. It all sounds good, but to many midlife men and women it's just not that easy.

Modern science is dedicated to helping boomers live longer and stay healthier, and the advent of medications such as Viagra, Levitra, and Cialis has created a new sexual awakening for middle-aged men, and a lot more headaches for some middle-aged wives. These medications originally developed to treat erectile dysfunction have become a life saving solution to those men who do suffer with the problem. For men who don't suffer, these medications have become recreational supplements to improve performance. (Although I do not think they are exactly screening middle-age athletes for using them.) For millions of men (and women), these small pills filled the promise of countless hours of satisfying lovemaking.

However, these pills offer little help in untangling the emotional and relationship pressures that frequently accompany middle-age confusion about sex. Women may mistakenly assume that it is no longer "them" that excite their husbands, but merely a chemical phenomenon, not an outgrowth of sexual attraction to her. Partners and wives can also feel that their sexual performance is not satisfying to their mates. When once may be enough, women often feel that they have disappointed their partners who are ready for a second or third round.

We know from some psychology or biology class we took along the way that human sexual response depends on a number of things: the interaction of physiology, psychology, and culture. Take a look at all of the factors that have influenced your sexual relationships as a young adult. Many of those same things still have an influence now on how healthy (or unhealthy) your sex life is. As relationhships change and as we age so does our desire for sex. I just caution you that before you or your mate start popping pills, try to discuss the reasons why you think you need them. If they are solid and acceptable to both of you then great. Make sure however, that taking Viagra or any other sexual performance medication is not masking the real reason behind your problem. The discussion alone is a great opportunity to communicate about your relationship on many levels.

INSIGHTS

GOING THROUGH "THE changes" (as our mothers and fathers used to call it) can be a physically and emotionally draining time. But it doesn't have to be that way. It is all in the attitude you want to take. I agree that waking up in the middle of the night sweating is not fun, nor is looking in the mirror only to find five more gray hairs—on your chin. Between feelings of fat and old, you may find that hormonal changes cause you to have less patience for everything—even those roles and duties you once claimed that you "loved the most."

Loss and change are a major part of midlife.

You may feel like you are losing it all—

but you're really not.

We may feel that our beauty has faded with our youth and we are no longer desirable. But research supports that women, in fact, are commonly expected to retain a strong sex drive well into middle age. For female boomers who want to remain sexually active, it's great that we are supported and validated. But women with less sexual desire or opportunity may feel inadequate and inferior, like they are missing out. Remember that sexual performance and desire during the menopausal years and afterward is not all about aging, but is about so many other major changes going on at this phase of our lives.

We need to view sex as one, but only one, of the elements that enhance our lives. This is a time in your life that you need the support and understanding of your mate, your family, and your friends. Educate them a little about what is really going on in your life. If you cry for no reason at least they will know why. If you are not "in the mood" your husband may not feel as rejected. If you look in the mirror and see those fine lines, think of them as lines of distinction. It is important to view the biological changes of midlife as a normal part of maturing. The fear of the unknown, of becoming wrinkled and ugly, of being useless and neglected, of being helpless and poor, or of having no one to take care of us has a tremendous effect on our self worth. Your childbearing years have come to an end but your life is not over, it is really just starting. Get fit and stay healthy for the second half of the journey.

4

WHERE DO I GO FROM HERE?

The Emotional and

Psychological Issues

~

BACKGROUND

*I*T MAY HAPPEN the first time you look in the mirror and catch a glimpse of gray. Or when you realize that you have just threatened your pharmacist with death if he does not have your prescription ready by noon, you may take a step back and wonder, "Who have I become?". Perhaps your kids, your spouse—or maybe even the mailman—have all noticed these changes before you did (but have cautiously elected not to tell some middle-aged maniac anything). As the frequency of these strange behaviors (and confusing new emotions) continues, you may begin to question everything about your existence. You'll find yourself asking, "Why now?" Why me?" "Why this?". It feels like the world that has been on your shoulders for the past twenty-five years or so is getting even heavier (and at our age we have to be careful about just how much we can carry). After spending half your life convinced that you know yourself better than anyone else, you come to realize that that is all a lie.

Just when we feel that we have lived long enough to know everything, we begin to realize that most of the great body of knowledge we have gathered is completely superficial. We have become experts at fixing our computer's hard drive, cooking low-carb meals that can be frozen for a year, or texting our bosses while we are driving down the thruway—but what did we really learn about ourselves? Most middle-aged adults believe they already went through this search for deeper meaning during their more explorative college years . . . and wasn't that enough? Actually, no.

Each stage in our human development requires a reevaluation, and each transition requires updated skills. Think back to how difficult you thought the search for inner meaning was in your twenties. (Actually it was so hard that it drove an entire generation to indulge in mind-altering drugs.) The difference between now and your twenty-something self is that by midlife you have not only gained knowledge—but more importantly—you have gained wisdom. This not-so-newfound *wisdom* gives adults the ability to deal with adversity despite ambiguity, and to successfully deal with hardships. It also enables you to step outside of yourself and be able to look at things from different perspectives and understand another's point of view (okay—you don't have to like it or adopt it as your own: just validate it).

The most important thing, however, that anyone must understand about middle life is that the journey from here on will from time to time be filled with loss, change, and letting go. I am sure you have already real-ized the "loss" part (because on many days I am sure you feel like you are "totally losing it", and in some ways you actually are). You may be losing your kids as they move off to college, or to a spouse as they marry. You may have lost or are losing an elderly parent—or even lost your job (to some twenty-five-year-old, no less). Everything seems to be changing so rapidly and life as you knew it is gone, but have you really changed? You may feel the pressure to change along with the times and circumstances, but feel resistant to give up what you once had. This is one of the few times I would suggest that you "go with the crowd and change."

Since all those things we had in our early adult years that have kept us "together" this far are gone, letting go of our *former lives* isn't easy. Sometimes, in fact, once we let go of these things that defined who we are, we feel like our lives will fall apart, and are afraid of who we might become. (You may have felt some of that "I'm becoming my mother/father" panic already.) But don't worry, that panic is temporary. Try to look at it this way: those people and things that have provided you fulfillment and security for a long time will never be forgotten, but in some ways, they will be replaced with new and different things. It is okay to cry when you kiss your child goodbye at the steps of their college dorm (or the altar), or when you pack up your desk for the last time (which you have probably wanted to do a hundred times throughout your career anyway), or when the "for sale" sign goes up on the front yard of the house, which is now too big without the kids anyway. This chapter will help you to spend some time getting rid of your emotional baggage and preparing for a journey into a new phase of life.

Before we begin, it is smart to understand

the stages of the transition that lie ahead.

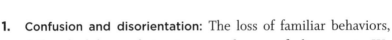

1. **Confusion and disorientation:** The loss of familiar behaviors, daily schedules, and structure may leave us feeling empty. We grieve for the loss of a familiar environment or relationships— whether that means Sunday evening dinners with the family, or going to work every day.

2. **Emotional, physical, and behavioral reactions:** We feel unusually anxious or somewhat depressed. Our energy and motivation to do anything becomes low. We find ourselves impatient with others and ourselves. These emotions and behaviors are normal responses to loss and each of us will react differently.

3. **Reorganizing and regrouping:** After some time, we begin to feel better and start to accept the change. During this stage, we typically find hidden strengths that help us take whatever action is required to move forward. This restructuring and reorganization of our lives leads us to deeper insights about ourselves, and we develop an expanded, improved identity, and notice an improved overall functioning. We often emerge stronger and wiser as this positive transition enables us to take control, adjust to change, and progress on the right track. As a result, we have developed the skills and confidence to be more prepared for

future changes (and I don't have to tell you that inevitably there will be future challenges).

How we deal with midlife depends upon

how well we can practice accommodation.

According to Carl Jung, our preferences are innate (they are with us from birth and not influenced by our environment), but what *is* influenced by the environment is our behavior and our perception of ourselves. And these are influenced by many factors—including our parents, siblings, other children at nursery school, how much and what television we watched, surroundings in our early childhood, and more. As a young child, we are eager to please and adapt to those around us in order to be accepted by them; therefore our perception of ourselves is molded in order to "fit in" with the various social situations in which we find ourselves, which Jung called accommodation. This process results in us presenting ourselves as different people in different situations.

However, many times, the way in which we accommodate to others goes against our own true preferences. There can be cultural, social, or environmental pressure to behave in certain ways, and these often conflict with how we view ourselves. Did you always hate being the charismatic corporate wife; or the conservative classroom mom? And many times, it can take tremendous energy to maintain these personae if they are in conflict with our true selves. For these people, midlife transition can sometimes be a difficult and painful process. Many people feel the solution to this is engaging in various stimulating or dangerous behaviors, or buying something new to make them feel excited again. However, this is just a temporary fix to the midlife change (see Session 5, The Midlife Crisis). It's important you understand that this transitional period is a normal part of life and getting older. Take a deep breath.

Midlife and its Stressors

One MacArthur Foundation study found that for midlife men and women day-to-day stressors like fights with a spouse, work deadlines, and financial pressures are more common than major life events (divorce or a loved one's death), and have just as great an impact on their psychological well-being—especially on women. Midlife women are asked to do more multitasking than are their male counterparts and report higher levels of distress as a result. (No newsflash here. Haven't we all checked in with the office while in line at the grocery store buying cake for dad's birthday dinner.)

Day-to-day stress doesn't add up to a midlife crisis. In fact, the evidence of these day-to-day and crossover stresses, may point to one positive part of midlife. The reason why midlife people have these stressors is that they actually have more control over their lives than earlier or later in life. When people describe these stressors, they often talk in terms of meeting the challenge.

There are many signs and symptoms that you may notice when you are experiencing stress and anxiety. These signs and symptoms fall into four categories: feelings, thoughts, behavior, and physiology. When you are under stress, it is not unusual to experience one or more of the following:

Symptoms

FEELINGS

- Feeling lonely or worthless now that the nest is empty
- Feeling angry, sad, and guilty that life is not the same anymore
- Feeling insecure about your future
- Feeling unneeded and unwanted by your children
- Feeling a loss of meaning and purpose in life
- Feeling old and unattractive
- Feeling worried about your family, your health, your marriage
- Feeling that you are "locked in"—and stagnant
- Feeling lost and not knowing what direction to take

THOUGHTS

- You want to—but are afraid to—reject the idea of what others think you should be.
- You undertake a self-appraisal and wonder *is that all there is? What have I done with my life?*
- You want a new identity: you want to become someone different.
- You want your marriage to change, or to change your partner
- You want to be young again.

BEHAVIOR

- Putting aside the old norms and rules, but you don't yet have anything to replace them; you are experimenting, searching, and exploring.
- Retreating to your old life: even if you are dissatisfied with that life
- Facing up to the undesirable aspects of your own character
- Understanding patterns, and longstanding relationships change. Finding new relationships as your lives, and your friends' lives, change.
- You can't adjust, have difficulty moving on, and can't seem to find a new path.
- You find it difficult to be a caretaker for your parents, children, or grandchildren.
- You may begin to hide your sadness by self-medicating and seeking feel good antidotes.
- You may lose your identity, feel trapped.

PRESENTING PROBLEMS

No More Security Blankets: Clinging to the Past

As we age, many of us develop a fear of aging and death. By clinging to the past and not letting go of memories, old rituals, and patterns, we can get stuck: we harden and resist, and may even miss opportunities that might bring about change, transformation, and fulfillment.

Change is difficult without a doubt. It is easier to stick with what we know and with what makes us comfortable. The problem is that sometimes those things aren't the things that make us happy. When we cling to the past—to the way things were, to our children, to ideas that are no longer appropriate, to mates who have died, divorced, or left us, to images of ourselves that have faded, to possessions, or to memories—we rob ourselves of the opportunity to grow.

Instead of focusing on our present life,

vast energy is wasted wishing for or reliving

history. As a result, our future is stifled by

obsessions with the past.

 Just Call When You Need Me

Begin by jotting down how many times a day or week you call or e-mail your kids who are away at school or who no longer live with you; or how many times you call your husband,

wife, girlfriend at the office. You can do this same exercise with marking down how many times a week you find yourself staring at photos of your child or flipping through old pictures of you when you were younger.

Take a look at the things and the times that you do this the most. You probably think you know what they are; but my guess is that you probably don't know *why you are doing them*.

- Log your clinging behavior and identify the antecedent (i.e., those events that occur right before you fall into past bad behaviors).
- After a week, look at your list of "antecedents" and see if there are any patterns. Most likely, you will discover that for many of the events on your list, there is some underlying issue that sets off your need to keep in touch. For example, you may notice that when you are bored you call your daughter at school. When you are overwhelmed about making a decision you call your husband at work. The real problem may be that you are feeling insecure or afraid to act independently.
- Address the root cause, *not* the actual events that have lead you to this behavior.

Lost and Found: Losing the Kids, Finding Yourself

You would think that by the time you lived half your life you would have cemented all those relationships with your family, friends, children, coworkers, and neighbors—and they would be around forever. However, just when you have the time to enjoy these relationships, they seem to start disappearing. Children move away to college, or marry. Friends begin to retire, or flit around the country visiting their children, new grandchildren, or ailing parents. Unfortunately, now that you are ready to embrace life, you are forced to "let go" of old routines. You may experience grief at losing a life you once led.

This type of grieving is different for everyone. Some begin a week, month, or year before the goodbye and others remain in denial and don't feel it for months, or years. There is no timeline that is right. It's been a lot of years of listening to noise, the fighting, the telephone, and the tears of your kids; many years of holiday meals at grandmas, and a lot of heart-to-heart conversations with your best friend over coffee. It's been a lifetime of hearing the comforting sound of a parent's voice (even the complaining) that gave you that instant connection to your own childhood. So why shouldn't you feel an emptiness and sadness when you have to let go, and say good bye to what was an earlier (and younger) stage in your life?

Midlife adults *do* need to take time to adjust to all the change, all the loss, and all the letting go. You may be letting go of old familiar roles and responsibilities, but are suddenly finding yourself gaining new ones— (coaching your children for that first big job interview) meeting new in-laws, planning weddings, anticipating the birth of your grandchildren. This is the time to reflect on your past and take a look at where you have been. Learn from your mistakes. Plan ahead with optimism and live your life as you imagine it.

LOSS OF PURPOSE

In midlife, people often find themselves suddenly questioning, well, everything. Have they been a good parent? Is their marriage all it is cracked up to be? Is their career meaningful? Does their existence on this earth actually help anyone? (Silly question: how else would your kid have ever won a prize at the science fair?) Nothing may be spared from this harsh self-examination. Self-exploration of your past achievements is a great beginning in finding new purpose in midlife. Inner questioning is crucial, and if a person hopes to achieve greater meaning and self-fulfillment, courage and a leap of faith may be necessary. It is easy during the midlife years to think your "job" on this earth is over. It is critical that you develop the ability to value and respect the life choices you have made and take responsibility for creating new ones.

Carl Jung, a psychologist and the foremost leader in the study of midlife transitions, believed that as we grow older, both meaning and purpose become equal. Both are needed to thrive. His teachings propose that early in life, meaning is derived through preparation for living. In later years, meaning is derived through an examination of the inner self. Jung identified five main phases of midlife.

Jung's Stages of Midlife

- **Accommodation:** meeting others' expectations—and this occurs earlier in life, as well as in midlife. (*I have chosen to forfeit my career to stay at home raising the children, which made my husband and kids happy.*)
- **Separation:** rejecting the accommodated self. (*I've been a devoted mom, but I'm no longer happy just staying at home.*)
- **Liminality:** a period of uncertainty, where life seems directionless and may meander. (*I want a change, but I'm not sure into what.*)
- **Reintegration:** working out "who I am" and becoming comfortable with that identity. (*I have started to volunteer my time and am going back to college to take a few classes—and I like it.*)
- **Individuation:** facing up to and accepting the undesirable aspects of our own character. (*The children are a little angry and my husband thinks I am selfish for not being so available as I used to be. I am finally putting myself first.*)

So, Really, What Is The Purpose of It All?

Try to fill in the blanks below with just a word or two, and then read each sentence to yourself out loud. Think about what you wrote. Try to figure out what you would have to do to add greater meaning and purpose to your life based on your answers. For example, if your most meaningful purpose in life is being a good parent to my kids, then consider how you can achieve that. This exploration may take you into some uncomfortable areas—however, it is absolutely critical to moving forward—and ultimately can be a very liberating experience.

1. The purpose of my daily existence is _____
   _____
   _____.

2. The meaning of my work here on earth is to _____
   _____.

3. I have been given the gift of_____
   and should be sharing this with my family, my friends, my
   community or the world.

4. I would feel great personal and deep satisfaction if I
   could help others by _____.

5. I cannot let _____
   stop me from reaching out to find my true purpose.

THE GOOD NEWS IS . . .

Midlife adults who take the time to become aware of, acknowledge, and embrace Jung's five steps, can create a midlife that is characterized by a sense of passion, awakening, and renewed spirit, including:

- A greater sense of integrity
- A feeling of being "more alive"
- An increased feeling of contribution
- A stronger psychological well-being
- An acceptance of their own mortality and, as a result, a greater sense of their life plans and meaning
- A feeling of greater control over their lives and a feeling that their life matters
- An increased sense of self-esteem and happiness

Live It Up a Little!

Sometimes by midlife you have lost the zest to enjoy life, and experience it to the fullest. (I know you don't have a lot of time but give it a try.) Did you ride motorcycles, run marathons, disco dance, play drums in a band, or backpack through

Europe? Make an updated list—a more mature version of these same types of experiences you have had lately now, during your midlife years. (Yes, the list is short, I am sure.) Now, think of how you can create that similar feeling of being alive and really experiencing life during your midlife years. Do you want to travel to China before your sixtieth birthday? Have you always wanted to study to become a chef? Have you always wanted to run a marathon? Anything is fair game, and definitely don't get inhibited with this exercise: you will find that many of the items on your "GO FOR IT" list are more attainable now that you are older.

GO FOR IT! YOUR TIME IS NOW

PAST _____

PRESENT _____

FUTURE _____

Not Feeling So Good About Yourself: A Declining Self-Esteem

So, you've worked your whole life to have the house you wanted, the career that you dreamed of, and the family that you prayed for—but now that you are on your own and your identity is no longer as strongly tied to any of these things, you may feel confused. In fact, many midlife adults often express disappointment, discontent, and boredom with life, asking themselves "Is that all there is?". It's not so impressive (or so we feel) that you once were the CEO of America's largest cereal company, or that the son or daughter you raised won an Academy Award (after all, it wasn't you that they interviewed on the red carpet). That huge house you might have boasted about before may now seem empty. And sure, you have money stashed in your IRA, but life doesn't seem to be about money anymore. Often, these changing roles can make us feel worthless, unhappy, and even worse invisible. Our sense of self-worth defines who we are, and self-esteem is a core identity issue.

Self-esteem is all about that annoying little inner voice that tells us how critical it is to be accepted, or will shout out all of your faults at the slightest provocation. Besides making you feel lousy, low self-esteem can also make you irresponsible: remain in a bad relationship, go on a shopping binge, have an affair, get into drugs (and yes, that means prescription medications, too), gain weight, or even go under the knife for cosmetic surgery. If you are feeling unloved, unattractive, or useless try to figure out why—and then change your perspective. Midlife is a time to take a look inward and reevaluate your worth based on a different set of standards.

A drop in self-esteem may be tied to your changing social networks, as well: The same people who helped shape you and made you feel good about yourself are no longer available to help boost your ego. That could be the parent you relied on, a boss who thought you were the greatest, and even the pizza delivery guy who once thought you were "hot" and tried to flirt. (Now you longer eat pizza because you're counting carbs.) So, then, who is really there to reaffirm that you are still important, still loveable, still smart, and still sexy? That becomes *your* job at middle age—and to do that, you must look inward at the qualities and attributes that make you valued and make you feel good about yourself.

Ageism is not a made-up word in our society like many want us to believe. Magazines, television, and ads for cosmetic surgery entice us to "repair" our aging bodies, as if the natural process of aging were an accident or a disease. The emphasis on youth, beauty, and thinness in our society is especially damaging for middle-age-women and men. Sure, you can parade around and tell people (and yourself) that you are older and wiser than those anorexic twenty-one-year-olds, but that still won't get you the job, or past the bouncer and velvet rope and into the nightclub. But the fact is that we really don't want to see ourselves twenty-one again, even if we choose to ignore all the stupid mistakes we faced back then. Think back to those days that you imagine were so perfect. You can quickly come up with a list of imperfections and negative thoughts you felt about yourself then. (And those probably aren't too far away from the same ones that are making you feel so bad about yourself today.) Remember that midlife is a time to look at yourself in the now, and decide what it is you want to be written on your epitaph.

Recognizing Your Inner Child

Most of us have an inner child. Thoughts, feelings, and behaviors that you had as a child still remain part of you. Your inner child may surface many times throughout your midlife years (and I don't just mean when you throw a tantrum because you're stuck in traffic). Allowing your inner child to "speak" can be healthy. Ask yourself the following and create your own inner dialogue that will help you identify which aspects of your life are influenced by the child that remains within you. Understanding where these feelings, thoughts, or behaviors came from will help you to better address them.

1. Are you bored with your life, your family, your job, with everything? *(Maybe as a child you were entertained constantly; and you had too much stimulation or not enough.)*

2. Do you find yourself seeking new ways to find a thrill in your marriage or romantic relationships? *(Perhaps as a child you were afraid of intimacy and sought only meaningless sexual encounters.)*

3. Do you feel like you are constantly searching for something to fulfill you? *(It's possible that you were never rewarded for your accomplishments, or you had parents who weren't there to meet your needs.)*

4. Do you feel burdened but unchallenged? *(It could be that as a child you were given too much adult responsibility; or no responsibility at all.)*

5. Do you feel discontent with portions of your life even though they once made you happy? *(Maybe you were never a happy child and have carried this unhappiness into your adult life.)*

6. Do you feel confused about the direction your life is going? *(Perhaps you were never good at making decisions—whether to join baseball or soccer; maybe no one was there for you to help you learn how to make decisions.)*

Facing the Obituaries

It happens to us all. One day, for no apparent reason you turn to the obituary section of the newspaper and begin to call out the ages of the deceased—as if you are waiting to hear your lottery number come up. All the while you are carefully seeing if, maybe, there is anyone's name that you recognize. You might deny it, but what you are really looking to confirm is that you are not as old as these folks (and that, don't worry, you have decades more to live). Once you've convinced yourself of this, you can go (happily) back to your morning coffee.

However, what is so difficult in midlife is hearing the news of friends our age who suddenly are ill, and are dying. Many of you might want to skip this section but please don't. No one likes to admit or discuss their own mortality; I understand it is hard. Your reaction to loss will in part be influenced by the circumstances surrounding it. The death of a loved one is always difficult, particularly when it is sudden or accidental. Your relationship to the person who has died will greatly influence your reaction to the loss. As many of us in mid-life begin to lose a parent, we also begin to feel that we are losing the most important part of our past. We grieve not only for them, but also for the place we called home and for the passing of our own childhood and youth. Recovering from such a loss takes time. Another challenge, though not often mentioned, is overcoming feelings of guilt about recovering from that loss and moving on with our lives. It is natural at middle age to look at where you are going—and it is just as natural to wonder how much time you have left. There is no time (according to my calendar) to let guilt stand in your way of moving forward.

Write Your Own Obituary

No, not because you fear what your family members might write, and this can be your final, controlling action on this green earth. Actually, taking the time to write your own obituary can be therapeutic, and sometimes, cathartic.

Limit your response to 500 words and write what you would like others to say about your life when you are gone. Most people are surprised to find that their own obituaries end up being more centered on people than on achievements and material things. (While you may have convinced yourself that being a super-CEO is everything, in reality, simple things like being a good mother, helping your community, or being remembered by your grandkids may be the truly important things to you.)

Depression is a Risky Business

In midlife, women can often become consumed by their partners', children's, parents', friends', and colleagues' needs and expectations. (Not a surprise, right?) This ever-present set of demands—that have nothing to do with your own wants and needs—can have long-term damaging effects on a variety of levels. At some point, every woman must take the time to carefully assess her life objectively, with realism and with hope. If she doesn't, she may find herself in the throws of depression, feeling utterly hopeless, empty, and afraid.

Also, some women are at a higher risk for depression during menopause, including those who have had undergone a surgical menopause, or hysterectomy; women who are separated, divorced, or widowed; and women with a history of depression. By recognizing what may trigger feelings of depression, you can cut it off before it can take hold and develop.

Who Do You Think You Are Anyway?

So things have changed and so have you. You may have wondered lately Who Am I? What Have I Become? But I doubt you have asked yourself, or really compared yourself to who you were when you were twenty, and thirty? (And if you have I would guess you only compared your waistline and dress size.)

Describe yourself by completing the following sentence in a *one-word answer*. For example: *I am quiet. I am a tolerant. I am angry. I am resentful.* Try to make a list of at least twenty-five. Sounds pretty easy. It's not. You may find it hard to admit to (or find) all your good qualities, or you may be too embarrassed to admit your bad ones. Either way becoming aware of who you are now can help make the changes necessary to become the person you want to in the future; or the person you once were.

Proactive Ways To Help Manage Depression

- **Get in the habit:** As we age, we do get set in our ways. And that can be a good thing. Regularity in our habits and scheduling becomes increasingly important during midlife. Remember that your body will respond to basic, minor changes in your health habits. If you begin to make small changes now, eventually these habits will become a priority. Be consistent. Exercise, eat healthfully, and sleep well. Why start now? Because if you don't, it will be difficult to change in later years.

- **Get real:** Think for a moment of how old you really are. Not your state of mind but your actual chronological age. While going for excellence is great—expecting perfection is not so great an idea. By now you have lived long enough to know that life can be hard and no one escapes disappointment and pain. No one is perfect, and nothing is perfect. We cannot fix every thing, person, or situation, and believe me any of us who are parents have tried.

Making peace with the concept that you can only do your best will add to a positive attitude and improve your mental health.

- **Get it together:** Recognize the importance of loving and being loved, including self-love. Middle age is a time that we tend to feel alone, and often lonely. Seek happiness by surrounding yourself with people who support your efforts, stand by your decisions, and offer unconditional love. Have the courage to set boundaries and distance yourself from individuals who downplay the person you want to become or who pressure you to compromise on your core values.

- **Establish strong social networks.** People who need people may not be the "happiest" people in the world; but they are a whole lot healthier than those who choose to become isolated. People who maintain social relationships during the second half of life also reduce stress and anxiety and depression.

Seek Support from Your Friends

If you find that you are depressed or discouraged by the aging process, stop complaining to friends that are just as depressed as you. Yes, misery loves company, but you will find yourself feeling a lot better talking to an older friend or relative that has been through the process and who can be an "older" role model, or the voice of experience. Look through a family album, and find that person whose look you like. Ask them about their secrets to aging. Remember: You share the same genes so maybe if things worked for them, they will work for you.

GOOD, BAD, OR OTHERWISE, STRESS IS THE ENEMY

Positive Life Stresses

Promotions, weddings, vacations, and all of life's major milestones can precipitate short-term depression in midlife women and men, or really to anyone. But at midlife there is so much else to deal with that middle age people are particularly vulnerable to negative effects of stress. We tend to be so blinded by the excitement that we see these events only as "positives" and don't realize the emotional toll they can take on our mental and emotional health.

Negative Life Stresses

Family emergencies, extended caregiving responsibilities, financial challenges, faltering relationships, childcare dilemmas, and workplace challenges can bring unhealthy levels of stress to our lives that can result in such serious illnesses as heart attacks and strokes. Enlisting (and lending) anticipated help before the next major landslide of stressful events is especially crucial.

ONGOING STRESS AND "HASSLES"

We seem to think that it will take something really big to create the kind of stress that, for a lack of a better choice of words, would "kill us." But that just isn't true. Each day we are faced with micro-stressors that cause us to become annoyed, aggravated, or just upset. Over time these become "hassles" and take their toll on our health.

Make It a Top Priority

Make another list. (What are you are kidding, my lists have lists). Until you can decide what is most important to you, inevitably you will waste a lot of time on things that are meaningless in the long run. (Okay, getting the dry cleaning back in time for next week's business trip is important; but not as important as being there to pick your father up at the doctor after his cataract surgery.) Define the priorities that are most important to you. Maybe you need to break them into daily, weekly, or lifetime priorities. Make sure before you prioritize your life that the things on your list are realistic and attainable ("lose twenty pounds," for example, in two or three months, not in a week). If not, you will set yourself up for failure. Then, for each priority, figure out a plan to accomplish that goal ("join a gym," or "begin walking thirty minutes a day" are examples). Without a clear plan to accomplish everything on your priority list goals are just daydreams. Monitor your progress and reward yourself for each goal you achieve! (That of course would be getting to cross it off your list and have one less thing to do tomorrow.)

INSIGHTS

GROWING OLDER ISN'T necessarily about decline. Even though many of us don't want to visualize ourselves getting older—and associate aging with walking hunched over with a cane—midlife can in fact represent the beginning of an increasingly higher quality of life. However, until now, it has been easy to believe cultural myths, largely negative, about midlife. There have been too few examples to counter those falsehoods. Check the shelves at your local bookstore. Other than a few clichéd titles about midlife crises, the topics bounce quickly from parenting to retirement, and then on to death and bereavement. It's as if middle-aged folks were invisible—but why? It may be because middle age draws focus on what we are not (young, thin, sexy, etc.).

You may feel confused and in fact, many midlife adults often express disappointment, discontent, and boredom with life, asking themselves "Is that all there is?" However, the fact is that we really don't want to be who we were when we were twenty-five. You weren't perfect then and most likely had some self-doubts and insecurities. Now in midlife these same thoughts become magnified in your mind.

Regardless of how you choose to deal with midlife, it is important to remember there is much to be gained during these years. Focusing on the more positive aspects of life can have a calming effect and lead to a clearer vision of the more important things in life worth exploring. Midlife is a time to realize that you no longer have to worry about conforming to what others want you to be; but rather you are free to be just who you want to be.

Remember that middle age can be just as fulfilling as any other life stage. In fact, many of my patients have reported that the happiest period of their lives is when their children grow up and leave home. They finally have room in the garage for the car, an extra room to put their exercise equipment, and time to spend alone with their spouse. They begin to see all sorts of possibilities that went ignored, or have been long forgotten; they report being more relaxed—and yet, more assertive. Likewise, for the men in your lives, the big change is often that they "rediscover" the relationships—career can become less of an "obsession" and the focus is returned to their loved ones.

Also, by challenging ourselves, we can forge the new connections needed for further psychological growth. If we can move beyond stubborn myths about the aging brain, great things are possible. Think about it.

Successful aging is not about managing decline. It's about harnessing the enormous potential that each of us has for growth, love, and happiness.

Remember, everyone goes through transitions as we age. Worrying about midlife is nothing to be ashamed of, but consider it an opportunity to explore and grow as an adult. You should have fun exploring and reexploring your life in new ways. And remember: Don't trap yourself into the thinking that you're too old, because you can do anything you set your mind to. Everyone deserves abundance. Take charge of your life and take action to grow spiritually and emotionally.

5

THE MIDLIFE CRISIS

Fact or Fiction

BACKGROUND

WE ARE ALL familiar with the term "midlife crisis." We may laugh and picture the 45-year-old man who goes out to buy a shiny new red Porsche (not mentioning that his four young kids at home may never get a ride). But a midlife crisis involves much more than a few unseemly decisions. A midlife crisis can occur at any time—whether you are in your 30s, 40s, 50s, or beyond. For many of us, it is a time when you stop looking forward to ordinary activities and suddenly feel bored with everything. And this can include your career, personal life, or even your free-time activities.

There are many triggers that can set off a midlife crisis. We may get overly concerned with numbers and statistics (*Will I be able to retire when I'm 60?*). For others, it is because of physical changes: We may lose our reproductive capacity, or lose our hair and acquire a little extra flab. New responsibilities are a common trigger, including children returning home to live, or leaving home for the first time; caring for aging parents, and new requirements and responsibilities at the workplace. Not to mention debt and the death of a parent. (And anyone wonders why we are over the edge?) As a result of all of these changes, many people start to panic and feel they have to reevaluate their life, job, and family—and make some changes while there is still time do it. In general, the term midlife crisis, describes the crisis that occurs when people stop thinking about their life in terms of things that we have years to deal with—and instead begin focusing on how much longer they may have to live.

The word "crisis" has become so popular in our overly-dramatic society, that to experience a midlife crisis may seem fashionable, totally acceptable, and even expected. The truth is that we have crises throughout our lives, and very few are age-specific. So then, is the crisis you're having now any different than any other crisis you've had? Honestly, no one expects you to stay up all night making love like you did when you were younger (except maybe the makers of Viagra). But do all these life changes really warrant you to remain in crisis mode for the next twenty years? Midlife only becomes a crisis when your inability to accept your age and the changes it has brought to your life becomes the source of severe depression, or appears to be leading to hastily made, negative decisions.

The midlife crisis has given us an exaggerated image of women and men acting as if they are teenagers, remaining in total denial of the fact that they are entering a new and more mature stage in life. Yes, middle age historically corresponds with a turning point, a time for that existential search for life's true meaning. (Sounds a little like what teens do when they get confused about their changing bodies, can't identify with the world at large, resist the increasing responsibilities of getting older, and generally "freak out.") For us, the interweaving biological, psychological, and social factors bring upon feelings that "our time has passed" and that we are just not as young as we used to be.

For women, the signs can be painful (emotionally and physically). The finality of the childbearing years and the realities of hormonal changes and age-related diseases make them uncomfortable and sad. Trips to the vitamin store and the doctor's office increase as they panic at the first signs that things are changing (only to find out that everything is "normal" for a fifty-year-old). Some women get depressed and feel they are no longer attractive, or needed. This can lead to depression as they take a close look and reevaluate their jobs, family relations, and values. They know where they have been so far, but are afraid of where the rest of their life will take them.

Men are human too (yes, they are) and therefore also experience the challenges and crisis associated with midlife—they just talk about it less.

However, for some reason the realization that something is different seems to happen all in one day, or one enlightened moment. It is not that little extra flab around the middle or those silver chest hairs that give it away: men seem to muddle around, somewhat aware that they feel "aimless," "confused," or "lost." They begin to question things they once believed in, like marriage, work, and friendships. Some notice that they are losing their vitality, joy in things they once loved—and that nothing really seems important. Like women, men start to think in terms of how little time they have left. Like women, the first jolt of serious bad news— the death of a parent, trouble in a marriage, a career setback, a crushing chest pain and the word "biopsy"—can set any midlife adult thinking about his own mortality.

What Exactly Is a Midlife Crisis?

Symptoms

FEELINGS

- Feeling isolated and alone
- Feeling chronic fatigue—exhaustion, tiredness, and a sense of being physically run down from balancing marriage, aging parents, and work
- Feeling depressed, anxious, tired, irritable, and moody as a result of hormonal and other physical changes
- Feeling burned-out and a general lack of caring or concern, appearing unmotivated
- Feeling fearful about the future and confused about your life
- Feeling apathetic and becoming withdrawn because you are overwhelmed by all the changes

THOUGHTS

- Losing your own identity and having no sense of who you are
- Thinking that your life has no real meaning
- Sensing a declining degree of marital satisfaction

- Wanting to change your job, your marriage, your friends, your everything
- Realizing that you cannot continue to compete with younger workers and younger women
- Looking at yourself with little esteem

BEHAVIORS

- Taking it out on the marriage—having an affair, leaving your spouse, or fighting for no reason
- Hiding your sadness by self-medicating, and seeking feel-good antidotes
- Exhibiting anger at those making demands of your time
- Criticizing yourself for putting up with the demands of others
- Finding yourself cynical, negative, and irritable
- Mood swings, going from peaceful to agitated, from loving to mean, from content to discontented

PHYSICAL

- Losing sleep and/or concentration
- Experiencing impaired functioning in social and vocational settings
- Gaining weight, losing stamina, having hot flashes
- Getting gray, going bald
- Becoming nearsighted; needing bifocals

Midlife Isn't All That Bad?

The belief that we all go through some sort of psychological trauma at midlife is not really true. Yes, we all go through many changes but rationalizing or justifying "misbehaviors" such as overspending or infidelity are just excuses that determined people use who just really, really want to do those things anyway (or for those who love them and just want to explain away their behavior).

The Latest Research Shows That Midlife Isn't All That Bad. And actually, you probably already knew that. Or at least you've realized that much of what we are *experiencing* at midlife turns out to be quite at odds with what the media *tells us* about this time in our lives. The larger, cultural message we receive about middle age is that we are on a constant downhill slide, but you may feel that your marriage is stronger than ever, stress bothers you less now than twenty years ago, or that menopause brings more relief than distress.

There are *enormous* dynamics in the middle years resulting from transitions like job change, illness, divorce or widowhood, remarriage, kids leaving or returning home, and becoming a grandparent. A midlife crisis is not for everyone. Actually, some people never experience anything resembling a midlife crisis. These people include those who constantly make adjustments to their life's path, never had a setback that challenged their beliefs about themselves, are extremely self-aware and able to handle life's upheavals better than the rest of us, or are generally happy in all important parts of their life. Even Erik Erikson (mentioned earlier and long considered the preeminent authority on adult development), changed his beliefs regarding the changes occurring in our middle and later years (not surprisingly, as he himself passed through those stages). Later, he came to believe that we are continually redefining our sense of identity, that identity challenges are ongoing, and that people change as they transition through the life span.

Surviving "The Crisis"

Does all this good news mean that we're no longer entitled to our own midlife crisis? Midlife is certainly a time of considerable change, but research now indicates that these changes do not necessarily result in chaos and trauma. To the contrary, positive attitudes and new possibilities can counteract the negative effects of midlife challenges.

Adopt a More Positive Attitude about Aging

When you were twenty, someone forty seemed old; when you were forty, someone sixty seemed old; now you are sixty, and you feel old. Have your views on what old "is" changed through the years? How would you describe your grand-parents, or parents to someone in terms of their age (really young, old and gray and grumpy . . . etc.)? The way we see age shapes how we view our own aging. Start focusing on the positive aspects of aging. Find a celebrity idol that is your age. Read up on them and find out what made them so successful, interesting or influential, or so attractive. Adopt some of their philosophy on life, learn about their health and fitness secrets, and work on developing a similar attitude.

INSIGHTS

MIDLIFE BECOMES A crisis when you can't cope with the natural and inevitable changes that aging brings. If you find yourself depressed, making irrational decisions, and acting like an irresponsible teenager, you just might be in the midst of a real crisis—one that you created. I am not saying that you created the turmoil, but maybe you are not taking the opportunity to discover the positive aspects of this time in your life. (And yes, there are positive aspects.) Justifiably, you are going through major changes in your life that you have no control over. But aging is about accepting change, and embracing new possibilities along the way. It's not a disease or an illness that needs to be cured (although some experts in health and beauty field may beg to differ).

Many of the physical and emotional symptoms that women experience in midlife are not new to them. Women have wrestled with their hormones since they were teens. However disruptive menopause can be, the most important changes are often emotional and spiritual, not physical. Spend some time talking to your midlife friends about what happens when they hit hurdles like divorce, disease, an empty nest, or the loss of a parent. You'll see that very often the result is a (pleasant) surprise, even to them. The old expression "what doesn't kill us makes us stronger" applies here.

Regardless of the course you take in dealing with midlife, remember there is much to be gained during these years. Losing some of the angst of youth can have a calming effect and lead to a clearer vision of one's self and their world. With the right attitude and inner resources, midlife can bring newfound freedom as you realize you no longer have to worry about being who others want you to be, and are free to be just who you want to be.

Midlife crisis symptoms bring to the forefront thoughts about what you don't want—but those same thoughts can just as easily be used to figure out what you do want. Focus entirely on those things. When you think about the life you want—not the one you have, the one that's trapping you—you feel stronger. Your mind does have the power to give you the best of everything in the second half of your life and you deserve it!

Tap into the power of your midlife crisis symptoms. Remember that seizing opportunities takes courage. Look at it this way, each new adventure you face is like a coin toss. Heads you win—tails you lose. You will either give yourself the chance to move forward and find your passion; or you will step back in the shadow of doubt. The choice is yours. If you fall back upon the safety of what you know best and pass up the opportunity to experience growth, you'll generally feel older. As you paint a picture of the life you'd like *next*, consider what would add zest to your life—and what will challenge you to stretch. Consider what have you always wanted to do—and the fears that have continually blocked you. Resolve today to face those fears, and go for it: At worst, you won't have to worry if life is passing by without you.

With that same sense of discovery and determination that boomers have brought to "timeless" experiences (including growing up, finding peace, or burning out), women are confronting the challenges of middle age and turning them into opportunities. Thanks to higher incomes, better education, and greater experience at juggling multiple roles, more and more women have discovered that there has never been a better time to be middle aged then now.

A Self-Assessment: Are You in Crisis Mode?

What's Not So Normal?

We all make impulsive decisions, want to turn back time, and feel a little down in the dumps as we face the many challenges of midlife. That is normal and that is okay. But whenever a behavior becomes an obsession and interferes with our social, emotional, or occupational functioning it is time to take it seriously and consider help. Be on the lookout for:

- Impulsive behaviors and poor decisions; financial, social, or career-wise
- Questioning the meaning of everything and being suspicious of everyone
- Searching for a sense of purpose; feeling the need to change the world
- Feeling trapped in a rut; or burdened over your job and responsibilities
- Feeling like time is running out
- Obsessing over having a youthful appearance

- Shopping compulsively for cosmetics and youth skin care products
- Increased reliance on addictive substances—alcohol, narcotics, prescription medications
- Getting lost in the past; fantasizing about the glory days of your younger years
- Depression—crying, not eating, not sleeping, withdrawing
- Focusing on thoughts about death, yours and others
- Experimenting with dangerous new activities; being involved in risky business

If you or someone you love is experiencing any of these midlife crisis symptoms now and then, take heart. You can find power in the crisis and turn it into triumph. Experiencing a midlife crisis means you're not happy with what you have in your life. It is a process of looking at what you have created in the past and thinking about what you want to create for your future.

6

MARRIAGE AT MIDLIFE

Live Happily Ever After

BACKGROUND

Do you find yourself asking lately, "Why did I even get married to begin with?" (That may echo the question "Why did we ever have kids?") For most of us, it was our natural desire to procreate and have a family of our own that drove us to marriage in our twenties or thirties. But with the large numbers of divorces today, these are serious questions for many. And although you most likely got married because you loved each other, you stayed married because of so many other reasons less romantic. The kids came along (or they were right there from the start as part of the package) and things changed. Your family grew and so did your stress (and debt). You did your best to keep everyone happy and never really worried about if you were happy or not—until now. Midlife marriages are often the toughest to survive and enjoy.

Many midlife couples find themselves becoming sandwiched between taking care of their children, parents, mates, and themselves (which by the way, always *does* come last). These demands can seem unlimited and unrelenting—making the two of you anything but "husband and wife." Today, midlife parents may have young kids of their own, be raising teens, or still be "raising" young adults—paying for graduations, cars, college, and/or weddings (taking a toll on your patience and paycheck!). There are many middle age parents who still feel very much young, but are actively involved with their grandchildren. And there is always added pressure from "outsiders" who admire your success and press you for your connections, volunteer time, or expertise in business or life.

This constant push and pull can make a midlife marriage seem dull and, often, as obligations increase so do the resentments. The time and the physical and emotional energy it takes for midlife adults to balance visits with mom in the hospital, visits with the kids at college, or visits with the grandkids for a weekend (not to mention taking time to attend board meetings, and doctor appointments) is exhausting. Individual needs seem to get pushed to the background, and you find yourself defining your marriage as a commitment you made "for better or for worse." In the back of your mind, you believe that there will come a day when the kids are grown and life together as husband and wife will get back to "normal." The problem is that you have been raising kids and living in chaos for so long you can no longer remember what "normal" is.

It is important to keep in mind that midlife gives you a second chance to create a different (and better) kind of marriage that will last "until death do us part." It is safe to say that most reasonably mature midlife adults will admit that they are not the same person they were as a teen or young adult. Most of us become (somewhat) less selfish with our goals and ambitions and seek to deepen our relationships with others. Women tend to become more mellow and assertive and seek deeper meaning in their relationships; no longer does cooking dinner for their husbands and volunteering to head the prom committee make them feel needed and important. Men in midlife tend to reach out to the relationships that they have ignored all those years (while they had a monogamous marriage to the office), and now want it *all* to be a success: work, the kids, and the marriage. But too often they find that some damage has been done and that they wish that wake-up call had been heard a few years earlier.

So now, if all this is true (and of course it is), then you have midlife women who are speaking up for themselves and who are out the door seeking new horizons, and you have midlife men who are homeward bound so they can spend more time with their wives and children. Needless to say, this may not be the best mix for a successful marriage.

This is a time to step back and begin to renegotiate. Make new demands on your marriage; be flexible and willing to adjust. You have come this far, and who knows, it might be worth it—since no one really wants to take that journey toward old age alone.

Symptoms

FEELINGS

- Feeling confused about what marriage is all about now
- Feeling misunderstood or ignored
- Feeling frustrated that your needs aren't met
- Feeling alone with a stranger after so many years together
- Feeling trapped in marriage you are unhappy with
- Feeling bored or that you've "simply had enough"
- Feeling that you have little desire for sex

THOUGHTS

- Realizing your new emergence as an independent and free woman is a strain on your marriage
- Wanting your marriage to be what it was when you were younger; or wanting your marriage to be totally different than it is now
- Believing that you are not attractive to your spouse, and that they prefer someone younger
- Wishing the children would be home again and everything would be better

BEHAVIORS

- Giving scornful criticism and becoming defensive
- Sending and receiving "mixed messages"
- Holding back information
- Shifting roles
- Insisting on equality with your husband now that the kids are gone

- Blaming your children for the problems you have had through the years

PRESENTING PROBLEMS

For Better and for Worse: Changing Marital Roles

Most of us looked toward our parents as role models as we were growing up. Good, bad, or otherwise we believed this was the way men and women, and husbands and wives should act. Until we grew up, left home, and saw that we had choices. Not so long ago, it was easy to identify what exactly men and women "roles" were. In our parent's generation, for the most part, women stayed at home raising children and running the household—and men were expected to be successful income-producers and providers for their families. But over time, our world has changed. As educational levels rose, so did expectations and the need for additional family income. Married women, even those with children, entered the workforce in ever-increasing numbers, which created ever-increasing dilemmas for women. Should they stay home with their children? Are they bad mothers if they pursue their careers? In the past, the guilt-free, no-hassle solution typically was waiting until the kids grew up and then taking your turn to pursue your own career and passion.

Today, our husband/wife roles tend to blur. Life gets complicated and there is so much to be done that no matter what your "assigned job" was in the past you find yourself doing your partner's job, as well. Moms who were traditionally "in charge of the kids" now find themselves enlisting dad to help with the headaches and heartaches of raising teens. And for both sexes, work in later middle-life begins to slow down—you approach retirement, and you have more time on your hands. But this feeling might not last for long. Grandmothers and grandfathers are now also being asked to help out caring for their grandkids. The days of mom and grandma in the kitchen baking pies while dad and grandpa are out fishing are pretty much history.

Today, women are less dependent on men as they move through the second half of life. By this time they have successfully met the challenges of changing, flat tires, jobs, and diapers (many have even changed husbands successfully). With the high rate of divorce and the increasing number of single women living alone, women face more of the kind of stresses that tend to bring on midlife crises. Many are equipped with the financial know-how, skills, and confidence needed to understand their frustrations and resolve them. But other women find themselves in worse financial shape, emotionally distraught, and lacking the resources to cope with the enormous pressures of midlife.

In some sense, women are having midlife crises now because they choose to. The support base and confidence they have built over the years—whether it is from soccer mom friends or corporate coworkers—has helped them realize their own strengths and has encouraged them to overcome their weaknesses. As the fear factor lessened and the risks of initiating change became reduced, these women in their midlife years desire equality and respect, and finally are no longer afraid to demand it. For other women the struggle is not so easy, but the need for change remains strong. Regardless of what resources or skills you may or may not have, your midlife years are the time to reevaluate what it is you want for your future.

REEVALUATE THE RELATIONSHIP

Most women have spent half their lives trying to figure out their relationships with men. Men, on the other hand, have spent half their lives avoiding thinking about their relationships. Then all of a sudden, sometime in the midlife years, men are ready to talk as they find an increased desire for intimacy and a deeper meaning in their relationships. (Hello: where were they when we wanted to have that conversation twenty years ago?) Oftentimes, men find increased intimacy or connectedness with their partners by learning to reframe their relationship to be one of friendship—others find a greater capacity for listening and empathy. But no matter what sudden (if unexpected) changes your partner makes, don't forget to address your needs, as well. These tips will help you do that.

Say I Do—Again

After so many years together you have learned what *"to have and to hold in sickness and health"* means—especially now—*"and in good times and in bad."* But you may have forgotten the other promises you made. Some may no longer apply and others might need to be added.

Write a new set of wedding vows. Include those commitments that you feel must be made to one another if you are to enjoy a stronger and healthier life together as partners, friends, and lovers. Bet they will be different from the ones you wrote when you were younger. If you happen to have those around compare notes. Doing this will give you the opportunity to discuss and commit to making the second halves of your lives together even better than the first. Create a celebration dinner, weekend, or picnic where you can read your vows aloud. This is a good time to reflect on all the reasons that you married in the first place.

It Takes Two: Share in Your Parenting Responsibility

Just as having children bought you closer together twenty or thirty years ago, the many trials and tribulations of parenting that followed can create distance and resentment between you. Rather than blaming your spouse for his lack of good judgment, try to lean on each other during disappointing times. Everyone makes mistakes. Children are not born with instruction booklets and all we can do is try to keep the pieces together the best we can. (So, you let your teenage son have the car, but it was Dad who gave the OK to let him take it to go skiing two hundred miles across the state.) You have made it this far and no matter what differences have come between you during your marriage, don't let the kids be one of them.

I know this chapter is about midlife marriage but with the growing number of divorcing parents, and the increasing research on the benefits of shared parenting; raising children together with an ex-spouse is a part of midlife. Yours, mine, ours, and anyone else's in fact. If you divorced when the children were younger (that meant you were younger too), then you may think things will be no different regarding the kids now. Wrong! When children reach their teens and young adulthood at the same time you reach midlife, new attitudes, insights, and relationships develop regarding parents and step-parents. Teens may want to make new "choices." So be prepared for the son that lived with dad all those years to decide to move back in with mom; or that the daughter who always resented step-mom to suddenly find a new friend in your ex-husband's wife. If you want your children to be happy, try to accept change.

Another stress on older marriages is the increasing rate of adult children returning home, called "boomerang children." It can be hard to turn them away when they are in need of financial support, especially while they continue education, make career changes, or adjust to a divorce. To minimize conflict and protect your marriage, establish clear understanding about roles and expectations *before* consenting to your adult children moving back in: Mom won't do the laundry, and Dad won't foot any more loans, and *they* will do the dishes!

You Can Plan On It: Marriage After Retirement

A smooth transition into retirement takes planning. This should be something to talk about now while your hearing and mind are intact. Be very clear about postretirement expectations of each other, and set boundaries. Because of extra time together after retirement, strengths and weaknesses may become easier to spot, and after all, menopausal women are known to be irritable and will not only spot your flaws but will remind you of them. It is just the two of you, so everything becomes magnified and the blame game is even easier to play. (After all, for the past thirty years could you ever really know who was responsible for leaving the empty milk container in the fridge?) Couples usually have a period of increased friction, but then are able to enjoy retirement. Midlife marriages can resemble your first years of marriage when everything was new and different—a period of change for both of you, filled with new adjustments and new joys.

SEXUAL INTIMACY

Intimacy in marriage includes not only the sharing of private thoughts and long held secrets; but also includes a physical bonding that comes from a healthy sexual relationship. Midlife can be a busy time, and can also be an excuse for your decreased interest in sex. For so many couples midlife marriage becomes a marriage of convenience, or of comfort. If you have not enjoyed a healthy sexual relationship for years now is the time to change that. If you want to continue the same healthy sexual intimacy you have shared throughout the years, it just might take a few minor adjustments to do so. (Of course, with your busy schedules, you may have to schedule an appointment with each other.)

GRANDPARENTING

Watching your spouse grow into his new role as grandparent can be a fresh way to appreciate his personality and characteristics. (You'll find that he never really changed and is still making the same silly faces and noises he did when your own kids were small.) But you will notice that the pony rides on grandpa's back don't last as long. Grandma still gets joy from baking her favorite cookies and letting the grandchildren decorate them, but now grandma will make them without the butter or sugar because she is watching her weight.

Don't Let it Slide: Declining Levels of Marital Satisfaction

When people first marry everything is new and wonderful (remember)? They learn new things about themselves and their partners and experience high levels of satisfaction in their relationship. By midlife, couples have inevitably faced conflicts—arguments and circumstances that potentially build up a history of negative emotional interactions that erode marital satisfaction.

People—and relationships—are always changing. What you had together as a couple at twenty or thirty is different now. And different doesn't necessarily mean better or worse, it just means different. Women who in the past have been dependent on men, are feeling good about the independence they gain in midlife and should not feel guilt about abandoning their old roles for stronger and more dominant ones. (It is okay for women to have a voice about household issues and finances, whether they have been the breadwinner or were home baking bread.)

When couples feel they have drifted apart they begin to lose the motivation to support one another's individual goals and relationship goals. Research has shown that spousal support for these goals affects marital satisfaction. On a more positive note, people who are satisfied with their relationships and support one another tend to stay married.

Watch Out For:

- **Criticism**—Instead of complaining about a behavior, you attack your partner's personality or character, usually with blame. When you list complaints about past behaviors you are suggesting a character fault, which isn't going to help matters.
- **Contempt**—Contempt is criticism that is intended to insult and psychologically abuse a partner. This reflects a negative view of your partner (and it hurts).
- **Defensiveness**—Defensiveness is a way of avoiding taking responsibility by denying responsibility, making excuses, and attributing negative thoughts to partners. When you become defensive you are again placing blame on your partner.

Are Your Needs Being Met? You Can't Always Get What You Want, But You Can Get What You Need

We sometimes think that because we have lived together so long we know what it is each other wants or needs. No one is a mind reader and being married does not qualify you as one.

Spend a week logging all the complaints that you and your spouse have about each other and your marriage in general. (*He never compliments me on my appearance; she always puts her parents needs first. He is never is on time; she is always criticizing my cooking*.) Make separate lists and don't share them right away.

Next, make a list of what you need from your mate. (Skip the request for a new sports car and one more pair of designer shoes: get to the real things, like attention, affection, and cooperation.)

Now create a list of what your mate needs from you. (Look beyond his requests for more jewelry, football time, gourmet meals, and back massages to things like support, compassion, and understanding.) Are your two lists compatible? If not, what needs to change?

HIS _____

HERS _____

DON'T RULE OUT A GOOD MARRIAGE

I Love You Just the Way You Are: You wouldn't yell at a friend if her house were messy (although you might gently suggest that if her coffee table was not so cluttered you could admire the wood finish much more), so try to take the same outlook the next time your husband leaves the living room a mess. In short, look past your partner's flaws and focus on his endearing qualities. (And if you look hard enough he has some.) So he might have left his ice cream dish on the table and not put it in the dishwasher. But wasn't it he who stopped on the way home to get your favorite ice cream?

United You Stand, Divided You Fall: When major differences in opinion come up, look back on your years together. Today, maybe you have less to disagree about (especially if the kids are gone), or more to disagree about because your faults are magnified. So what if you don't always think the same? You are not the same. You have different strengths, which together can help you reach difficult goals you couldn't achieve on your own. Maybe he is a great negotiator and you are a great researcher. The combination could get you a great deal on the car that you always wanted—so don't fight it.

Think About Change— Didn't You Promise "For Better or For Worse"?

No one is perfect, but when it comes to our spouses we expect (or at least want) them to be.

Are there things about you that irritate your mate? Are there things about your mate that irritate you? (If you answered no to either, you are lying.) Identify those irritations and see if any can be changed. Think about whether or not you want to change them. If you can and want to change them—then by all means do it. If they can't be changed, don't feel guilty about it, just learn to deal with them. This is called acceptance, and it will be one of the most mature things you can do.

Who Do You Love?: The Midlife Affair

It is common to get bored with any relationship. That's not to say that your mate is "boring," but many midlife couples often feel that the excitement is gone. Many midlife couples realize that a huge part of the last twenty-five years was tutoring their kids in spelling, devoting their life to the PTA and to their jobs—and now the only excitement they share together is putting out the recycling or watching TV. You find yourself waking up wondering: *Who is that old guy (or lady) next to me? When did they get so gray?* You're exhausted getting out of bed in the morning after long nights waiting for the call to let you know that your daughter has gone into labor, and may find yourself longing for the kind of exhaustion that comes from late night hours of intimacy with your spouse, filled with laughter and lovemaking. While these feelings have been present off and on for years, marriage and fidelity often become part of a midlife assessment. The midlife crisis is not an "excuse" to have an affair, but the dissatisfaction you feel with so many things right now may be the reason you believe that you can justify having one.

Midlife women tend to define who they are by the role that they have played for so many years as mother. Men, however, define themselves according to the professional role they have held. Midlife is a time to scrutinize the part that each partner has played in the marriage. I have found that couples don't want to do this until there is a problem, or a threat to leave, or an uncovered indiscretion of their vows. Midlife marriages are sometimes hard to survive. But before you can move forward to improve a marriage, consider: Are you a good wife? Is he a good husband? Are you and he good lovers? Ask yourself if you really know what the other needs. Many women and men in midlife claim that they "don't know each other anymore," but are suddenly in shock and disbelief when they find out that the other is having an affair. After so many years of marriage it is easy to ignore the signs that something is really wrong; and the last thing you want to believe is that your spouse would even consider an affair, let alone have one. But once you are through with denial, look carefully at what went wrong and learn from it.

The older guy with the young girl in the sports car is no longer the envy of everyone at the golf course. These relationships have been the brunt of jokes for years and seem to denote a man's shallow need for sex, confirmation, and validation of his virility and youth. Why else would they do this—when they could be at home having a deep and meaningful conversation with their wives? As convenient as it is to chalk it up to hormones, that's not really fair. If a marriage has been ignored and a couple has not made an effort to keep themselves connected to each other throughout the years, temptation for another often pulls them apart. Midlife couples must examine the nature of their relationship to help them understand how one or the other has reached this point, or why they are feeling the urge to break their sacred vows of fidelity. Why are they so unhappy?

For many middle-aged men, a midlife crisis is precipitated by his own emotional state of confusion and his preconceived notion of what life will be like with a pre- or postmenopausal mate. Meanwhile, women going through menopause are encouraged to reinvent themselves and follow their dreams. This becomes a problem if her dreams include a man who is far younger, affectionate, attentive, and sensitive than the one she has now. Larger numbers of women are having midlife affairs than ever before and are turning traditional sex rolls upside-down. For both men and women, affairs take on a powerful exhilaration that is in sharp contrast to the pressures and stresses of the childrearing years, the new responsibilities of becoming caregivers to elderly parents, and the constant climbing of the corporate ladder. All of a sudden someone understands you, listens to you, and really cares (so you want to believe). Women particularly, and often subconsciously, see the affair as a way to reaffirm that they are still attractive even though their childbearing years, and their youth, is coming to an end. (Of course, the man she is having an affair with isn't exactly interested in fathering her children.)

Large events seldom destroy marriages—rather it is the little everyday stuff that makes or breaks relationships. Failing to communicate effectively, too much self-righteous posturing, bullying attempts at control, unilateral decision making, broken promises, and withdrawal from emotional and sexual intimacy can each alone cause a marriage to disintegrate. However, there are also several major events that can devastate a marriage: abuse is one; having an affair is another.

An affair is commonly defined as sexual relations outside of marriage. However, this can be too narrow a definition: it fails to acknowledge that marriages can be threatened by any relationship (sexual or otherwise) that attacks the bonds of intimacy and trust between spouses. A purely platonic friendship with someone outside the marriage can hurt a marriage if that friendship becomes overly intense, intimate, or invasive. Actually, any outside relationship that drains one spouse's ability to attend to the emotions, sexuality, or intimacy of his/her spouse, is a potentially damaging affair (for example, online chatting and cybersex can be real affairs capable of damaging marriages). Do not confuse this with the affair that you image your spouse is having with their Blackberry, Mac, or PC.

One frequent motivator for a person to have an affair is a quest for newness—whether from a need to diminish midlife drudgery, a desire to explore what sex is like with someone else, or an urge to recapture the sexual highs of earlier decades. Sometimes people are seeking to fill unfulfilled emotional or intellectual needs, and occasionally sexual dysfunction in the marriage contributes to affairs. (Men with erection difficulties or women who can't reach orgasm may seek out new lovers to prove that the sexual problem is their spouse's doing—and partners of those with sexual difficulties may seek out reassurance that they are still sexually vital in the arms of someone else.)

Often, an affair will have ripple-like reverberations on the couple's entire relationship. A straying partner may be unable to respond sexually to his or her spouse because of guilt over the affair, fatigue from juggling two sexual relationships, or a negative comparison of the spouse with the new lover. If the spouse discovers the affair, he or she is likely to withdraw emotionally—which can deal a fatal blow to a relationship. However, it's possible for a marriage not only to survive infidelity, but also to grow from this painful experience. To do this, though, both partners must face the personal and relationship issues that may have contributed to the affair. Couples therapy is a good place to turn for help in doing this. Sex therapy can also be useful if the affair has caused or resulted in part from sexual problems

However, the problem is often not with you, your spouse, or the relationship: It can often be simply the need for better communication. Take the time to communicate with one another about what you are feeling. It's normal and it's okay to question your marriage at this time in your life. After all, midlife is a time when you will be questioning the meaning and purpose of everything else, so why not take a deeper look at the relationship you have with your spouse? You have more time now to spend getting to know each other again: Don't be strangers. The words "alone together" probably haven't entered your vocabulary for years. I know after a decades-long rush of having kids, raising them, building careers and a home—and everything else—there hasn't been much time to be alone as a couple, but now is a good time to make that a priority. Midlife relationships, if you let them, can often blossom with age and can give you the courage to meet the demands and challenges of the years ahead. The intimate knowledge of one another that you have gained over the years creates a strong, enduring alliance that can weather many a storm.

You Can Talk To Me About Anything. Really?

It is important to open up a dialogue (and this can hard, especially at this time, since you are probably used to talking in the car, dropping an e-mail from the office, or shouting across the dinner table to each other). When one spouse starts realizing that "something is going on" and begins probing and demanding explanations, the straying partner probably doesn't understand it him/herself, and resentment can build. Here are some tips for connecting:

1. Don't ask "why" questions: they demand explanations and accountings. Often the person in the midst of a midlife crisis or affair doesn't know the answer, which adds additional fear and angst. Ask a questions starting with "why" and you get defensiveness. (*Why don't you listen to me? Why did you cheat on me? Why are you shutting me out?* If they knew WHY they probably wouldn't be doing it.)

2. Don't start off by asking questions at all: Start by sharing what you are seeing and experiencing, say that you understand he/she must be struggling, and that you want to support them. (*I sense that you are turning away from me, and are not interested or receptive in spending time with me alone*, etc.)

3. Focus on conveying that you are not demanding answers but that you want to understand what they are experiencing. (*Maybe if you explain to me more about how you are feeling lately, I can understand why you have been acting this way.*)

If you don't get an answer, try again another time. And Keep Trying. This not a one shot deal.

SAFETY FIRST: PHYSICAL AND MENTAL ABUSE

Sometimes both spouses are to blame for a failed marriage; they can assume responsibility and either end the marriage or repair the marriage. But in the case of an addicted spouse, an alcoholic, or an abusive spouse the issues are far deeper and more difficult to resolve. This behavior is usually something that middle age women have put up with for years, but felt they couldn't do anything about. *Where were they going to go? Who would take care of them and their kids? Where would they live?* These same questions and fears are shared by women of all economic backgrounds and from all walks of life. Although they see ending their marriages as the last resort to end a bad situation, middle age women often find themselves not financially, mentally, or physically fit to endure the escape. They can lie to themselves, and after the children have moved out they can lie some more. Physical abuse may be easy to spot. It is the mental and emotional abuse that so many women hide—out of fear and shame. Domestic violence and abuse of any kind should never be tolerated and most likely won't end. My advice is to seek help—fast. You have a whole second chance for a life that you deserve.

INSIGHTS

YOU SHOULD FEEL better knowing that all midlife marriages go through change and that the difficult times along the way are not necessarily signs of a "bad marriage." After reading this chapter, you probably have a better understanding of the complexity of midlife marriage—and you know that this phase of your relationship can be physically and emotionally draining. Just thinking about the work involved in maintaining a happy marriage and staying put in that marriage seems exhausting. You might even be wondering "Is it really worth it?" Many men and women feel stuck in a midlife marriage thinking there is nowhere else to go (and who would want me at this age, anyway, if I did leave?). With obligations to the kids, and to the bank on that mortgage, many midlife couples feel now is not the time to split up, no matter how unhappy they may be.

I also know that not every romance can be rekindled, nor can every marriage be saved. Years of neglect, unmet needs, stress, pressure, and poor communication can erode the solid foundation your marriage was built on. Midlife can also be a time when some are left alone as the death of a spouse or divorce cause them to assume roles they never expected. (These are issues discussed in Session Seven.) However, you are getting older (and wiser), and should realize that your future will always take with it a part of your past. As you begin a new journey into the second half of life, you can decide what good things about your marriage you want to pack up and bring with you—and what excess baggage you want to leave behind. This is your marriage—not your mother's or sister's—so don't look ahead at "how they ended up." Look back at the rough spots and the mistakes and see this as a chance to redo things.

Always remember that marriage is a partnership. Maybe it has not always been the 50/50 partnership you had hoped for—but as a team you have accomplished a lot together. At a time when many midlife men shift their needs toward their families and relationships, they feel confused, afraid, and at a loss of control. Men have traditionally been in control of their marriages; however, the women they married in the '60s and '70s were raised one way, and are now reaping the benefits of the women's movement years later. But no matter what roles a woman has assumed in the past, at midlife she has the opportunity to change or to make the choice to stay with the one she has. Both men and women in midlife begin recognizing that they are at height of their own control and are fully in charge of making empowering changes and redefining roles they have played throughout the marriage.

It is scary to think that at this time in your life—when you are losing your children and your parents—there is a chance that you can lose your husband to some younger, thinner woman (who may have firmer breasts, but has half your wisdom). What is critical is that you understand that you can reevaluate and reestablish the deep intimate connection that brought you together in the first place. Affairs are one of midlife's many wake-up calls. They force people to question, "Just what the hell am I doing and thinking?" But don't believe for a minute that the affair "just happened one day." Most are a result of years of discontent and dissatisfaction. And while no one "deserves it" because they were a bad husband or wife, they do deserve to understand what went wrong. Unfortunately, we tend to repeat the bad patterns of our lives over and over again unless we can heal fully and understand our behavior.

Midlife is a time to wake up and smell the roses (or at least notice them as you pass them by rushing to catch the train to work). Most likely, the years leading up to midlife have been so busy for you and your spouse that you haven't had time to think about what direction your marriage is heading—not to mention time to reflect on whether or not you have even enjoyed the ride. Sure, when an argument breaks out you are reminded of the marital flaws: You kiss and make up, all is forgotten (for the moment), and routine life resumes quickly. But midlife is the time to look at you and your spouse and really think about what your needs are, and if they are being met. This is a time in your life that things can become "about me"—about time, correct?

7

DIVORCED, WIDOWED, AND NEVER MARRIED

Me, Myself and I

BACKGROUND

JOU UNDOUBTEDLY BEGIN to hear yourself mumbling four-letter exple-
tives at the doctor's office when the next box on the intake form asks:
Married? Never married? Separated? Widowed? What business is it of any-
body's anyway? Many men and women feel pressure that by midlife they
should be married because that is what people do. However, on any given
day, being "unattached" (as my grandmother's generation used to call it)
has its positive and negative sides. Some of us will feel angry because we
have been married and it just didn't work out. For many other middle age
adults, feelings of sadness surface because they have lost their spouse to
illness. Whether being single at midlife was or was not a choice—and no
matter the cause—feelings of loneliness and a loss of sexual intimacy,
security, and family are common. Being single in a very couple-oriented
world can be difficult for midlife men and women who feel that they are
the third wheels in a world full of bicycles built for two.

The reasons that we marry, or partner, stem from a deep biological
need to mate. However, it is no surprise that as generations have changed
so have societal values: Making babies or having sex is not the number
one reason for most marriages anymore. But one thing that has stayed
the same is the hope and desire that when you do marry it will be forever.

In their early years of a relationship, young couples (like you once were) feel that love will last forever and take the words "until death do us part" seriously. And when we find ourselves alone in midlife, we can become unmoored: this wasn't part of the plan. (At least I haven't yet met anyone who just wanted to get married for a few years—or until their spouse gets old, out of shape, and uninteresting.)

When first faced with being alone at midlife, many individuals feel an empty void, unworthy, unattractive, and alone (or thrilled if they ended years of a bad marriage). There is no partner to talk to, no one to share their most private thoughts with, and no one to make them happy. Often these midlife adults fear dating, or their bitterness stops them from moving forward toward new possibilities and potentials. The temptation to look back is far greater than to look ahead. However, we can draw strength from the fact that we all started out single; and lived alone in our own worlds, bedrooms, or apartments at some time or another (okay, I know it's not the same but we learned a lot from those experiences). We survived our early years and most of us thrived. Through growth and independence we figured out what made us happy and what did not.

Midlife adults have the capability of gaining new independence and new visions for their future. As they look ahead to the second half of their lives, most realize that they do not want to spend it alone. Most are willing to give love another shot; only this time on their own terms and with the help of technology. They cannot envision another night at a singles bar making idle chatter with other lonely losers, so they turn to online dating services, and matchmaking websites. (Keep in mind however that those people in the bars and on the web are not necessarily losers, and by being single you are not a loser either.)

Without a doubt, "Till death do us part" remains an enduring vow for millions of long-married American couples, and the benefits of a happy marriage go without saying. But I know many of you are asking yourself just exactly what those benefits are? Men and women who have spent decades with the same spouse will give up marital security if their marriage has been an unfulfilling one. Today, the people ending long-term marriages after age fifty are one of the fast-growing demographics for divorce.

Not surprisingly, then, there are more "players" out there than ever before. Our higher divorce rates, longer life spans, and increased trend toward never marrying contribute to the fact that of the approximately 100 million Americans over 45, nearly 40 percent are single.

Symptoms

FEELINGS

- You feel alone, lost, and sad
- You feel helpless and hopeless
- You feel unattractive and old
- You feel bitter and angry

THOUGHTS

- You are facing the realization that you have no partner there to take care of you
- You believe that someone else should be responsible for your happiness and you can never be happy alone
- You envision the rest of your life without a partner
- You struggle with self-blame
- You think that every couple you look at has a perfect partner and happy marriage

BEHAVIORS

- You stop socializing in group activities
- You begin to spend more time with your children
- You avoid your married friends
- You complain and criticize dating and marriage

PRESENTING PROBLEMS

Happiness Is in the Eye of the Beholder

The common expression "happily married" has no universal definition, since happiness is different for everyone, and so is marriage. Some
believe that if you are married then you should be happy, others feel that
in order to be happy you must be married. Research even goes as far as
to suggest that married people are happier. (But then again research says
the same thing about people who own pets.) Happiness is not something
that we learn but something that we feel. No one can "make" us happy
and no one can "make" us sad (that is something we seem to do for ourselves). The question should be, "What makes us happy?" not "Who can
make us happy?". Whether you are married or single in midlife, you will
most likely find the need to begin reimagining your idea of happiness.
However, if you have been married throughout young adulthood, you may
have expected your spouse to be responsible for whether or not you were
happy on any given day. You may have even held your children responsible for your happiness or unhappiness. (They won the spelling bee and
you were happy; got kicked off the baseball team for fighting, and you
were unhappy.) I have heard it said, "Many parents are only as happy as
their most unhappy child." (*Makes sense, right?*) However, for you, now
things have changed. Maybe you are single for the first time in twenty or
thirty years, maybe you are married to someone who just doesn't "make
you happy" anymore. Maybe you have never been married and think that
having spent years looking for Mr. Right you have missed out on "true"
happiness. Midlife is the time to realize that you are responsible for your
own happiness.

No matter how independent and strong you may think you are—*are
you really happy?* Some of us have been independent and on our own
since childhood. Others have been encouraged from early on to become
independent. Some were given no choice but to fend for themselves.
Even highly accomplished women, contrary to popular belief, often need
someone else—and it's usually a partner—to affirm their self-worth and

make them feel worthwhile. Single women who were never married sometimes think that marriage would be the answer to all their unhappiness. Men have never been taught to question if they were happy or not, and if they did think about it, they certainly were discouraged from talking about it. Hopefully, both sexes are now slowing down and realizing that no one else is responsible.

When our marriages end, or when we realize that we may never marry, and we will enter our golden years living alone—we have to give up the idea that someone else is responsible for our happiness or unhappiness. We are forced to confront the realization that we have no partner to take care of us. Accepting these truths is hard; yet it is so self-affirming. It gives us the power and confidence to shape our own lives. We learn that we can tackle anything that comes along. Newly divorced or widowed women may learn to do their taxes, to take a more active role in household repairs, and to manage their finances on their own. Many women have been doing these things throughout their marriage and will continue to do so happily or not. Hard as it is, taking on new responsibilities builds our sense of mastery. Learning to create our own happiness is a difficult task, especially after twenty or more years of believing that it was our responsibility to make *everyone else* happy. So, you finally have realized that cooking dinner for your husband's boss or becoming homeroom mom isn't what really made *you* happy. The understanding is that once you define what it is that makes you happy; you have to go after it yourself. The independence and autonomy that comes about at middle age is powerful, and provides you with the time to really "regain"—or gain for the first time in your life—the happiness that you want. And still have the energy to bring joy (not happiness) to others.

I Can Do it Myself, Thank You: No Partner to Take Care of Us

Many women complain throughout their marriages that their spouse is "not listening to a word they say." (Sound familiar—actually, how many times have you said that *this week?*) But once they are alone and realize that there is no one to ignore them (or for them to complain about) they quickly begin to feel a new and painful emptiness. Anger is a common emotion felt by women (and men) who are left alone, no matter what the circumstance. If it's a bad marriage that ends in a divorce, you are angry with him for letting this happen; and probably angry at yourself for not being a better wife and making the marriage work. When a spouse dies in midlife, before you were able to grow old together, there is no way to be prepared. Likewise, if you are not married by forty or fifty, you may fear that no one will ever marry you, and you are doomed to be alone for the rest of your life (and some women are quite happy with the idea).

You may tell yourself that you will be all right alone. (You've done it before—well, maybe not since you were eighteen.) Your friends and family will help you through it, you try to convince yourself. At first, you are eager to accept all the invitations for dinner, movies, and barbeques with friends—but then, after a short while, you may begin to feel out of place. You may even avoid the supermarket because ordering chicken for one is too embarrassing.

In the long run, most women consider singleness, whether widowed, divorced, or never married, as a life filled with loneliness, longing, discrimination (in a coupled world), extra chores, and a sense of unfulfillment. The following tips will help you counter some of the feelings you may be having.

Look on the positive side: Living alone means you are

in control of the remote and the thermostat.

You may not realize it at first but you are now in charge of your own life, which is something you should have been all along. You abdicated your personal power to a husband who made decisions for you and the family. As a result you were happy (so you thought) because that was one less thing to do on your busy list of chores. But now look at the positive side, you no longer have to consult anyone to help decide whether it will be eat in or take out, or what cell phone company to go with. It is the convenience and comfort of having a partner around to help make these trivial decisions that women miss most at first. But they soon get used to this freedom. When it comes to making bigger decisions, however, they often feel a sense of relief and power immediately. For the first time in twenty or thirty years they feel as though their voice is heard and they can make their own decisions. (Like investing in real estate instead of antique cars, or turning the garage into a gym.)

If you are feeling bad about being single this exercise will remind you quickly of the nice things about running your own show and being your own boss

Spend a week making *no* decision on your own. Call a friend or a parent and ask their advice. Do the same for making social arrangements. Make a list of all the decisions you sought help with.

1. _____
2. _____
3. _____

Which things was it nice to have help with? Which did you find annoying? (Like trying to get a straight answer, or trying to get an answer at all.)

_____
_____
_____

We start out accepting singleness, but then something happens, often in high school, and society and our own biological drive tell us that we need to be partnered. Internal messages evolve, and at the same time we are pressured in a variety of ways by our friends, parents, acquaintances, and society. As more and more of our friends change from single to couple (whether via dating, engagement, marriage, or partnering) we begin to blame ourselves for not having a partner, start feeling left out, and wonder when our turn will come.

Who Knew It Wouldn't Last?: Coping With a Divorce

The married person never really plans on being single again and when this happens their world, as they have known it, ends. The emotional, social, and financial impact of divorce at midlife is different than if you were younger. It causes a greater sense of loneliness and a loss of self-esteem—whether you wanted out of the marriage or he did. If your husband left, you might feel that there is something wrong with you as a woman or as a wife. If you left the marriage, you might question your judgment in your choice of partner, or question whether or not there is something wrong with you for being so discontented or disenchanted with your marriage after all these years. Some women feel their lives have been uprooted. They often must sell their homes, give up family ties, and even leave jobs that they love to seek ones that will better help with their financial struggles. Many women find that they must go back and join the workforce after years of being a "stay-at-home mother." They may find themselves lacking skills to get a well-paying job. Divorced men may find themselves supporting two households or, if their wife has left, trying to fill a strange new role of being an only parent. Divorced people also have a social dilemma to deal with: some of the friends they had as a couple suddenly become former friends. On top of all of these problems, there is a loss of physical touch and sexual expression.

Sometimes the end of a love relationship can bring up powerful, even frightening memories of earlier separation or loss. The current crisis can prove more difficult as that earlier fear surfaces, be it a parent leaving for work or the loss of a first pet. The most recent statistics say at least half of all marriages end in divorce, so chances are good that you will either get divorced or have a friend or family member go through this ordeal.

To recover from the trauma of divorce, you have to understand the injury, apply the proper medicine, and allow enough time for the healing process to be completed. This is a kind of recovery therapy that only you can control—the results are up to you. If you shut yourself away from others and do not get out into the world amongst people, you will be lonely. To be happy, enjoy life, and know love, you have to make yourself available to other people. I know this is sometimes easier said than done.

The divorce is finally over and you're officially single, but are you ready to start dating again? While it may be tempting to get involved with someone new, you need to proceed with caution and not get involved too quickly. Give yourself time to get over all the bad feelings from your marriage, because old habits and expectations will color how you relate to someone new.

Until Death Do Us Part: The Death of a Spouse

The person who is single again because of the death of their mate experiences many of the same feelings that the divorced person does such as loneliness, a loss of home and family, and disorientation. There is also the social dilemma of being single when most of one's friends are married, a loss of sexual closeness, and financial stress.

The widowed person, like the divorced person, may also wrestle with guilt or remorse wishing that they had done more with their mate or had said more—that they had taken that extra trip. They wish they had spent more time with their mate instead of being preoccupied with things that now seem insignificant.

STAGES OF GRIEVING

In her book *On Death and Dying,* Elizabeth Kubler-Ross identified five stages that a dying patient and their loved ones experience.

They are:

- Denial (This isn't *happening* to me!)
- Anger (Why is this happening to *me?*)
- Bargaining (I promise I'll be a better person *if . . .*)
- Depression (I don't *care* anymore.)
- Acceptance (*I'm ready* for whatever comes.)

Other researchers who have described this process include:

- Numbness (Lowering of mechanical functioning and social insulation.)
- Disorganization (Intensely painful feelings of loss.)
- Reorganization (Re-entry into a more "normal" social life.)

No one term is better than another to describe what you are going through, and no one has a completion date for grieving. Just be aware what you are feeling is normal.

Still Looking for Mr. Right: Google Him

People who have chosen not to marry or who have never met the right mate experience many of the same feelings that the divorced or widowed person experiences. However, the most common anxiety expressed by long-term single people is thinking of themselves as misfits. They may struggle with sexual problems or a sense of being "temporary" in this world, but the most troubling feeling is one of low self worth because "I am unusual, I am unmarried." Many find themselves with the added pressure of defending or explaining their sexual orientation to people who assume they are not married because they have a same sex partner hiding in closet. (Are these people living under a rock?) However, if singlehood continues to grow as a viable and respectable alternative to marriage, the gap in happiness between married and never-married persons will also continue to close. In the meantime, however, for those who never marry, the following ideas may help you better cope within this world designed around marriage and children:

Examine How You Interact with the World Around You— Look Outside Your Window, the World is Waiting For You

- **Focus attention on the positives in your life and minimize focus on the negatives. You have been through a lot, or**

you may be at a new stage in life and have a lot to think
about.

- Make yourself available to others and begin to care for
them. Look for opportunities to be hospitable and nurturing. Remember that loneliness is something we create.
Loneliness is only a state of mind.
- Remember about half of the population is single.
Numerically you are not alone. Most of the feelings associated with being a misfit or lonely are due to a sense of
low self-esteem.
- Create a place that reflects your personality and is truly
a home. Singles often live "temporary lives." (No more,
"Later, when my situation is more stable, I'll fix up my
place.")
- Develop your own traditions and rituals, especially holiday experiences. Make your own memories that challenge your creative side.

Singles Seeking Singles: Dating in Midlife

As I mentioned earlier, there are more singles out there than ever
before. Increasing divorce rates, longer life spans, and a greater tendency
to never marry are yielding more single Americans than at any other time.
And now, we have more creative ways of finding each other, too. While
our generation has already created a boom of dating services, personal-ad
platforms, and singles vacations, the recent Internet explosion has made
looking for Mr. Right online as routine as shopping for groceries (but not
as satisfying). At midlife we are constantly being challenged with how to
use new technology in work and our personal lives. It can be frustrating
to try to get your e-mails forwarded to your office, or get your cell phones
to download directions—and now we have to try to get a date online.
Good Luck!

Likewise, as being single later in life becomes the norm, the stigma
of being "out there" is rapidly disappearing. People today speak about
their dating adventures as if describing a trip to the corner supermarket.
Corporate execs have no problems posting their pictures on an online

site, and newspapers detail dating success stories in its weekly wedding announcements section.

PLAYING THE FIELD (AGAIN)

No matter how long it has been since you have been single, dating again is just not as easy as they say it is—and the people that say it is easy are usually the ones who are married. It is not that dating is that difficult, it is just scary. With the possibility of rejection, loss, and heartache—why *would* we want anymore of that than we already have? Hey, if you really thought that way you would have never had children or gotten married the first time. Begin to realize that you have survived and grown from many risks and relationships that were worth taking a chance on. Love a second time around just may be worth the effort.

Before you go out on that first date, decide what qualities you are looking for in a potential partner, companion, or lover (trust me, this will prevent heartache and hurt feelings). Be clear about what you are looking for at this stage of your life. Once you find someone who possesses these qualities; or who has the same need as you do, go out as friends first: that way, at least you have the chance for a good friendship, even if nothing else evolves. It is possible that men and women can be friends without having sex, contrary to what we see in the movies. For many reasons as people enter into their midlife years their criteria for what they are looking for in a partner changes drastically from what they found attractive twenty or thirty years ago. Being hot, sexy, and smart is not half as important to middle age men and women as finding a partner who is healthy, kind, caring, and fun. *(But hot and sexy wouldn't be bad either.)*

If you have younger children still at home, then midlife dating becomes a lot more complicated and a lot more difficult. Your criteria and your expectations for the person you date are affected by your responsibilities as a parent. With the number of divorced men and women in our country the likelihood that you will date someone with children of their own is almost certain. This can be a good thing or a bad thing depending on your situations (and of course how good, bad, or wonderful each of the children are). You must begin to date gradually if you still have children at home. When you do begin to date try to be sure that this person meets your needs and is not just filling in for an absent ex-husband or ex-wife. Also make sure that you are not dating for revenge. (If you have experienced a bitter divorce this is tempting). Your children are going through a tough time also, so go easy on them if they routinely *hate* everyone you are dating. Remember it is just the idea that you are dating that they hate.

Begin by setting time aside to just be with your kids, and later, with friends. When you do begin to date, your children won't resent you for spending time away from them. Also, try to keep from making your home a revolving door of new dates. Kids—whether they are toddlers or teens—are still kids, and can easily become insecure and jealous. When you feel like you have met someone special (and you will), introduce him or her gradually, and only for limited amounts of time, as children may resent sudden changes in their routines. Throughout the dating process, spend individual time with your children so that they don't feel pushed aside (or worse, worry about losing another parent).

While you're probably not as carefree as you once were, you are probably a lot wiser. That's good, because it takes time and patience to begin dating again. Try not to rush things with any new relationship or to fall in love on that first date. Give yourself time to see if your feelings are real and if the relationship has any potential. Eventually, sex with someone new can be especially thrilling, thanks to the novelty and stimulation of a new partner.

INSIGHTS

WE NEVER REALLY know how life will turn out, but we spend our lives hoping for the best. No one ever marries assuming it will be temporary, and those that never marry feel the opposite: they assume that their "single condition" is only temporary and some-day they will find true love. In midlife you are halfway through the game, and you can dwell at what is behind you, or choose to look at what is ahead. For those who have lost a spouse, gone through a divorce, or never found true love, it seems like time has run out and the odds of being alone are overwhelming. It is easy to give up on finding happiness, but remember you have the ability to find happiness from other things in life that bring you joy. Think of the best times of your life—before you were with your partner. I am sure there were things you did by yourself that you enjoyed, that made you feel happy. And let's be honest: there were probably many times that your partner was by your side and they could do nothing to make you happy. You had to find your way by yourself—and you did. You knew then what made you happy and you went for it (maybe one of those things was ice cream, but now I'd suggest that—with your slower metabolism—you go for something else.)

It is easy to assume that love will never resurface, especially if you are widowed. But it does: many men and women in their 50s enjoy a serious, exclusive relationship after divorce—often within two years. For many, getting on with your life after a divorce or the death of a spouse means dating again, but don't do that until you are ready. Your ability and readiness to date and get "out there" is something you only have to prove to yourself (if you choose) and to no one else. Don't believe your friends and relatives who tell you that if "you don't date" you are stuck and not getting on with your life. Instead, focus on other things that are helping you to move forward. And if you are not doing anything to move on, you should be, whether it's going back to work, getting back on the tennis team (or if you were never on a team, joining one now), or signing up for a volunteer organization.

You may find that your single life after a divorce is satisfying and fulfilling in ways you didn't imagine. Women usually have more friends to support them after a divorce, and find it less lonely than do men. In no way am I saying that the end to a marriage is not painful and lonely—it usually is. But it is also a chance to find out many things about yourself that you never really knew. Be more flexible and open-minded about the kind of life you want to rebuild. Be realistic about your expectations.

Sometimes because you are familiar with a life you have lived, you find it hard to envision yourself living a different one. Finally, finding a different type of mate or a different type of lifestyle should not be seen as disrespectful to a deceased spouse, or an insult to an ex-husband (you did get divorced for a reason).

8

MIDLIFE ADULTS AND THEIR KIDS

It's a Family Affair

BACKGROUND

THERE HAS NEVER before been a generation of parents so invested in the success of their children, so involved in their intimate lives—and so afraid to let go. Baby boomer parents and their young adult children share so many of the same values and goals today (not to mention clothing and hairstylists) that parents can easily lose sight of what is best for themselves and their children. This overidentification does not develop only from the intense love and admiration that they feel for their overachieving, overwatched, and overconfident offspring, it also springs from a yearning for their own youth.

After years of following signs on the highway (which usually lead to ballet lessons, soccer games, and the mall), the natural course of human development at midlife should be a time for individuals to finally have a chance to travel in their own direction, However, today, the primary goal of baby boomer parents is the emotional fulfillment of their offspring (commonly called echo-boomers).

When we attempt to answer why we aren't happy, middle age parents use the excuse that we are exhausted from years of consoling our kids, financing our kids, driving our kids around, and worrying about our kids. Sure, parenting is definitely a lifetime job but let's face it: Once your kids are grown, shouldn't they be doing some of these things themselves? The problem is that baby boomer parents complain about how financially and emotionally dependent their adult children are on them, but when their children stop calling (for a day) or stop asking for money (for a week), they feel rejected, sad, and unneeded. The more we think of our children and ourselves as "equals," the more devastating the loss is when they finally move out and begin lives of their own.

However, for many boomers, an increasing number of adult children—more so than at any time in our history—are living at home longer, or returning home after being away for years. For these parents, it seems that just as they are done moping around the empty nest wishing that they had six more loads of laundry and three more cars in the driveway to annoy them—their children return home—perhaps alone, but often with a girl-friend, spouse, or occasionally even toting a diaper bag and grandchild. (You've told them that the door is always opened and they took you up on the offer.) Where are they supposed to sleep, since you turned their bed-room into a home office with a flat screen TV? Where will you work out, since the guestroom is filled with exercise equipment and a Jacuzzi?

This chapter will help boomers get a grip on their complicated rela-tionships with their kids, and prepare them for life as an in-law and (gasp) grandparent.

Symptoms

FEELINGS

- You feel sad and empty and unneeded when they leave home
- You feel needed when they return to live at home
- You feel guilty and confused because you are enjoying some "independence"
- You feel old because you have married children, or are a grandparent
- You feel bored and lonely because you don't have anyone to take care of
- You feel insulted that your child "wants" to leave home
- You feel worried about how your children will do on their own

- You feel like your life has been wasted. All the hard work and devotion to your children—and now *what about me?*
- You feel sad because the role you have loved so much is changing

THOUGHTS

- You think you are a success or a failure depending on how your kids turn out
- You are determined to have an authentic, intimate relationship with your children
- You just don't want your adult children to grow up
- You desire to be close with your kids—and have a yearning for your own youth
- You feel a competition with your children, trying to prove you are still young

BEHAVIORS

- You aren't letting go when you ought to—impeding your children's adult independence and also hampering their own post-parenting lives.
- You try to solve your children's problems for them
- You micromanage their lives
- You work hard at becoming friends with your child
- You constantly call them or e-mail them or travel to visit them

PRESENTING PROBLEMS

The Empty Nest Syndrome: Spread Your Wings and Fly

You knew it would happen someday, your precious children would grow up and "leave you." But think about how this really sounds—"leave you"—as if going off to college or moving out of the house was a form of intentional abandonment. While you may feel that in midlife you are dealing with one loss after another, keep in mind that things could really be worse: you could lose them for good in an overseas war, or temporarily lose touch with them while they are in rehab. (How does college or marriage look now?)

Like most boomer parents you probably have been saving for their college tuition since your children were born, and have had them wearing your college alma mater's t-shirts since day one. You've gone to every college-prep and high school graduation meeting—just to be sure that none of their classmates have an edge on your child. But when they finally get their first acceptance letter you feel mixed emotions. And when your child jumps with joy that he is "leaving" home you can become overly sensitive and even insulted. (*Why is he so happy to leave us?*) Ironically, when your child shows the slightest trace of nervousness at the reality he will be on his own next year, you feel like a failure for not raising an independent, well-adjusted child: You just can't win. In short, this is a time of huge change for you, your child, your marriage, and your family, and nothing seems to make sense.

Perhaps you make plans to redecorate, take a long-deserved vacation with your spouse or your girlfriends, or even think of going back and taking a few college courses. But mostly, you put all of these things off: You find little meaning in what you are doing, and the only thing that gave you purpose is gone. You feel like you have been terminated from the most important job of your life—being a mother. (Actually, your job is never really over, and you will still have those nights where you'll definitely be working overtime when your son or daughter calls at 2:00 AM freaking out over final exams, or is distraught and needs to be consoled over a bad breakup.)

There are no timelines and no rules about how to handle the empty nest. After all, when you love someone you want to share their daily lives, interrogate them about school, and hear for yourself that they are okay and life for them is good. (And with the help of modern technology you will still hear it all even after they are gone. And you will also pay a high cell phone—and finally learn about e-mail and instant messaging—to do so.)

Understand that not all parents (or children) react with overwhelming sadness and grief when they leave the nest. The relationships between the child and parent that existed prior to the "move" will be a large predictor as to how the separation will affect each. Of course those children that are highly dependent on one parent or another will have a more difficult time adjusting to decisions on their own. Parents who have been dependent on their children for support and companionship will feel more alone. If children have lived with parental conflict or circumstances that are generally difficult, they may actually be relieved to move out and start a new life. One thing that many children do (no matter how well-adjusted) is create a "hostile" environment prior to leaving home. They pick fights, become rebellious and intentionally obnoxious—just so the goodbye will be a little easier to handle. Think about it; isn't it easier to say "Thank goodness I am gone from my annoying family" than it is to say, "It is tougher to leave those loving and wonderful parents of mine than I thought it would be." Don't contribute to making that hostile reaction worse: This may be their way of saying they love you and they care. Always remember that you are the parent and they are the children: They need you and always will. You have had your chance to be on your own and live your own life. Give them theirs.

Remember:

- They may choose a different path in life than you would have wanted: Continue to point them in the right direction. (*If you don't they will find it hard to find their way home.*)
- Your role will shift from manager to mentor: They want to hear your opinion and will seek out your advice when they need it. (*But don't be upset if they ignore it.*)
- You taught them what they should know: Otherwise, they could have never developed the skills to leave home in the first place. (*And don't feel if they return home to live it is a reflection of you.*)
- You will always be their parent: They will always love you and need you. (*Especially when they are in trouble.*)
- Give them permission to make mistakes; and they will be less afraid to try new things. (*As long as the mistakes don't cost you money, of course.*)

- Let them figure things out on their own, rather than from you nagging them. (*I know it's hard not to when they still haven't filled out the change of address form and you are still getting their mail.*)
- You are their anchors and they need you. You'll always be their parents and they'll always be calling for help. (*Wait, isn't that the phone ringing now?*)
- They have observed you as role models and have learned how to successfully navigate life's challenges. (*Where else did they learn how to get the best table at a restaurant?*)

Repeat: *They Have Their Lives and I Have Mine—* Perma-Parents and TheirChallenges

From a psychological perspective postparenting years are a time for parents perhaps to reconfigure their identity : to relocate, change careers, join community groups, and reconnect with friends. Remember that this stage of development is your last shot at creating a life you want to live. (And you no longer have to take a "family vote" on it!) Today, however, parents spend a large portion of this time trying to help their children with the transition into adulthood and are robbing themselves of opportunities ahead.

Besides hurting their own development, are these parents helping—or hindering—their children's autonomy? Perma-parents, as we call them, don't really want their children to grow up. Why? Part of it comes from the acknowledgment that they, also, are getting older. And it is easier today than at any time before to stay connected to, and in control of, your children when they leave the nest. Cell phones, text messages, and e-mail can and do keep you in touch with their every move. Wireless services have given us all permission to intrude anytime we like. And since we are all very capable multitaskers, we are skilled at holding down jobs, going to the gym, and managing the lives of our children from hundreds of miles away.

Midlife parents who day after day secretly wish that their children would move back home to live should be careful what they wish for. Young adults are returning home in increasing numbers and parents are finding themselves faced with financial and parenting responsibilities all over again. This can put a tremendous strain on marriages, especially if one or the other spouse does not agree with the child's move back home. Financially, middle age is a time that people consider retirement, make plans to let up on work, and use their nest eggs to enjoy themselves. But when adult children return home, they can feel drained emotionally and financially—robbed from enjoying this new stage of life. Still others welcome their children back for the wrong reasons. They are alone, or see the addition as an opportunity to have some help with the household finances. But whenever the decision is made to allow an adult child to come home, be sure to set boundaries and treat them like an adult—not as the same child who lived with you when they were fifteen.

Let Go Already!:
Parents of the Echo-Boomer Generation

For a variety of emotional, social, and demographic reasons (including a desire to be close with their kids, a yearning for their own youth, or increasing divorce rates) many of today's baby boomer parents just don't want their adult children to grow up. (That would mean that they themselves would have to grow up.) Boomers may be the first generation for whom their children's emotional fulfillment and well-being is their primary goal. Unlike their parents, baby boomers so intensely feel they must raise a happy, responsible, well-adjusted child that they sometimes fail to raise financially responsible independent children. They feel guilty if their children have to struggle. (As if having your child sharing a two-room walk-up apartment with no elevator or dishwasher is the ultimate sign of poor parenting.)

While the generation gap used to be a significant barrier to communication, today's fifty-something parents are finding that—for better or for worse, and no matter how weird it may sound—they have many of the same core values and needs as their twenty-something kids. However, this identification with adult children means that parents often lose perspective on what is best for themselves—seeing their kids' successes and failures as their own and thus trying to immunize their child against failure. (In fact, many parents see the well-being of their adult children as one final parental exam.) These parents are told by the analysts (financial and otherwise) that their children and the entire "echo boomer" generation might not do as well financially as we do. And boomers don't want their kids to rough it. Emotional and financial dependence is a two-way street and boomers are clearly participants.

Perma-parents also suffer financial and emotional repercussions. The empty-nest years are a critical time for adults to save up for retirement—not pay off their child's college loans and credit cards. We have already discussed the fact that the postparenting period is a great opportunity for parents to reconfigure their identities. Having an adult child lurking around the house and feeding off the parental nest egg robs parents of some of this latitude, and these parents end up blocking their own transition into a new period of adulthood.

What Have We Created?

Whether you call them echo boomers—or "Generation Y" or "millennial"—they make up nearly a third of our population. They are also a reflection of the frenetic pace of change in our lives over the past twenty years: They are the first generation to grow up with computers at home, and 500-channel TVs. They are overachievers and overprogrammed, with cell phones, music downloads, Instant Messaging, PDAs, and more (that we pay for). They are completely plugged-in members of a growing global community. We are not far behind trying to keep up with the latest technology so we can keep our jobs, and stay in touch with our children. This generation has become our role model teaching us how to technologically communicate and keep the dialogue going between generations—even if it is through text messaging.

It should come as no surprise that they act this way. From before they can remember, they were buckled into car seats and sent to some type of organized group activity. After graduating from kid karate or pre-school, (that's right, I said "graduating") they were shuttled to play dates and soccer practice (actually, that was soccer practice on Monday, Tae Kwan Doe on Tuesday, religious classes on Wednesday, and so on.) These kids have grown up with structure, and dare I say it, a sense of "mission."

Likewise, this generation has long aimed to please—whether it has been their parents, friends, teachers, or college professors. Overall, they are in some ways very different than their self-absorbed, egocentric baby boomer parents. When you ask kids today, "What do you hope to achieve?" they respond, "I want to be good team member" (whereas ten years ago, it was "I want to be the best.") As a result, parents feel that their kids are delicate, almost fragile. And so it is no surprise that boomers tend to protect their children, inflate their egos, and fight their battles for them. Think of how much energy and time this has taken. Don't you think by midlife we should give it a rest and let them do some of this work?

Becoming "In-Laws" or "Out-Laws": Marrying Off the Kids

You are in midlife and feel that everything is disappearing. The kids have moved out of the house, your marriage as you have known it is gone, and you have lost one of your parents recently. Now when you need your children the most they are packing their bags and heading to the altar. You feel like you are *losing* your son, or *giving away* your daughter. But really you should be happy. As daughters-in-law and sons-in-law and grandchildren get added to the family tree, your life becomes full again. Your family is growing and this time you have more time to enjoy them all.

The jump from being Mom or Dad to being the mother-in-law or father-in-law is difficult for most parents. You didn't expect that you would feel this way. But it is common to be confused about what your new role and relationship with your child will be after the marriage. Will they still stop by for dinner on Sundays? Will my opinion still be welcome? Will they still join us on the annual family trip to Florida? Suddenly a whole host of unresolved issues and emotions surface, and they are often brought on by the stress and excitement of the wedding. It is important to understand that these feelings didn't develop in a vacuum. Ongoing issues with your other children, your husband and/or ex-husband, and issues from your own personal life become more pronounced as the "wedding" becomes one more thing to worry about. Most children marry at about the same time as their parents are beginning to take on new and changing roles themselves. So much is going on—retirement, taking care of their own parents, and the empty nest all seem to come at the same time. These changes are all normal, but it all may signify an incredible loss and change.

Many years ago, when your child left for college to live in a dorm with *strangers* that you knew nothing about, the excitement of that day was mixed with the sadness that came with realizing you were no longer their entire world. Yet, the deeper, underlying psychological issue was that you were realizing you were no longer *in control* of their whole world. Aside from moving away for college, your child's wedding is the most important milestone in their autonomy.

EMBRACE CHANGE

Look back at all the changes your child has gone through. First they wore long hair and ripped jeans (sound familiar to anyone?). They had friends you didn't like, and teachers you loved and they hated. As teens they kept their distance, and once they got their driving permit you became close again—literally. Then later their taste matured and they needed your credit card to buy that first interview suit. Remember those hours of alone time on the highway when you had their undivided attention? Those times are gone now and they are cruising life's highway with someone else. Recognize that letting go is a natural part of life. Consider your own life and how many changes you have gone through over the years and how things are changing for you now. Okay, you probably were not as hormonal then, and maybe you did not cry as easily, but still change and loss is as difficult as it is inevitable. Recognize that your child, too, has to move on—and that in many ways, the more his or her life changes, the fonder your place in their heart will be. In fact, you should be proud that your child is taking this great step forward.

Who Is That in the Mirror?: Recognition of Your Own Aging

It isn't really the fact that your child is marrying that makes you so sad; but it is the fact that you are old enough to have a married child. Were you that upset when your child became of legal drinking age; or when they were old enough to vote? Probably not, because those events did not reflect on how old you actually were. (I have never in fact seen a patient become depressed because their child turned eighteen and could now vote). The fact is, they are still your children and they still need you and love you. After the wedding is over they will need someone to turn to for advice about things that only people over forty know. (Like how to file a claim with the insurance company), and they will still need to know that unconditionally you love them when they have their first lover's quarrel (but don't expect that you will ever know about it but the suspicious call *just to say Hi*, on a Sunday morning at 8:00 may be a clue). They aren't really totally grown up yet, and you are the mature one so be proud that you lived enough years to enjoy the fruits of your labor. (And anyone that has given birth knows that is the truth.) Deal with the fact that we, as parents, are getting older, and so are our children.

THERE IS A LEARNING CURVE

Remember, too, that your child has enough stresses affecting him or her already, and so do you. Try to do your best to deal with yours without adding to theirs. Getting married is new to them and they are unsure of what they are doing. Having a new son- or daughter-in-law is new to you and you are not sure how to act either. This is a learning experience for everyone. Expect mistakes will be made, learn to say you are sorry, and learn to forgive. Moving on is part of the natural progression of things; this isn't something that you haven't handled many times before, and with success.

As parents we have lived our lives, have planned our own weddings, and have chosen our own spouses. In order for your children to learn and mature they need to have their chance to do the same. We can only hope that they will make the right choices for themselves (which by the way, may not be what you would have chosen). Support them and be a good role model. It is okay, and probably a good idea, to let your children know that at times your irrational or unexpected behavior is not necessarily attributed to their wedding, or to them; but rather to everything else going on in your life. Don't burden them with the details, not now, just make them aware.

Be sensitive to your new role of in-law. Competition may surface with your daughter- or son-in-law if they think you are interfering while they establish the ground rules in their own relationship. Try to develop a separate friendship or relationship with your new daughter- or son-in-law. The average age for marriage in America is now twenty-five for women and twenty-seven for men, so they have years of personal history to share with you. Get to know them and find out more about their childhood, their family and relationships with their relatives. Ask questions, listen to the answers, and remember them. Share stories about your family and your history as well. Remember your new daughter-in-law or son-in-law is part of your family now. Don't expect them to behave or think like your own child would, they come from a different family and you did not raise them. They have had different experiences, traditions, and maybe even different customs. Telling them about yours and learning about theirs will help create a sincere bond.

Being a Grandparent Can be Grand (and Not So Grand)

You just got used to the idea that your child has married and like the idea of having more children. Now, the news arrives that you are going to be a grandparent—and that definatly makes you feel old! We boomers pride ourselves on doing things differently, like taking chances and finding new ways to tackle problems. And unlike our own parents, we will probably have a difficult time accepting the designation "senior citizen"—in fact, the notion of being a baby boomer and grandparent just sounds wrong. Think about your own grandparents. Do the words "cool," "young and hip," "political activists," or "corporate CEOs" describe how you view them? Most likely, you just think of them as sweet, loving, kind, patient, little old ladies and men who can sometimes be a bit grumpy (and even little nutty).

Of course midlife parents expect they will be grandparents some day—when they are old. The problem is that today's midlife parents never want to get old, and once your children have children—you can definitely be viewed that way. But the number of second marriages, interracial, intercultural, and interreligious marriages is creating a very diverse population of grandchildren. As a result the traditional roles of grandparents need to be redefined. What are you supposed to do if your new son-in-law has children from two previous marriages—do you buy them all birthday gifts? If your grandchildren are being raised in a religion different from yours—does that mean you have to go to pray with them in another church? Can they come to yours? If your daughter has remarried and his parents are also divorced, what do the grandchildren call all four sets of grandparents? (Grandma #1 and #2?) It might sound silly, and the answers might sound easy—but let me tell you, they're not. These are the kind of issues that tear parents and children apart.

And now baby boomers are becoming the new generation of grandparents. However, we are younger, more educated, and more involved with our children (and of course our grandchildren) than earlier generations. Although this sounds like only positive intergenerational bonding, there may be some drawbacks. Your kids may not want your involvement with the raising of their kids. Remember, you devoted your lives to raising perfect kids—so in theory, they should be totally capable of raising perfect grandchildren. (So now when we question our children as to why they are putting our six-month-old grandchild to sleep without a blanket in 35 degree weather, they take it as a personal attack. Because we never criticized them growing up (we wanted them to be secure and confident!), we find ourselves having limited input and more conflict with them in regards to the raising of the grandchildren. This all creates a lot of pressure for us to stay quiet, and pressure on the children to raise perfect kids like themselves—making for potential conflict everywhere.

On the flip side, with so many children needing their parents' help in the raising of their own children, parents have the opportunity to play an important role in their grandchildren's lives. Our kids may be working late and can't get to daycare on time; they fly around the country on business and need help on the home front. However, you may be still working—and very much devoted to your careers—and feel torn by the desire to also help your children in any way you can. If it all happens right, you, as a middle-aged parent, should be well on your quest for deeper meaning in life and already be slowing down and taking the time to savor the important things in life. Grandchildren are an excellent excuse to force yourself to take that extra time off, or they can make you stop and think what it is you want from the new life ahead.

While the time demands of grandparenting can be stressful, it can provide an additional sense of purpose, aid your growth, and contribute to our overall well-being. A growing number of studies suggest that such behavior has positive effects on our physical health, too.

Adjust Your Attitude

Becoming a grandparent doesn't have to mean that you're "over the hill." Embrace the qualities that make our generation special and share them with your grandchildren. You'll be surprised by how much they appreciate it—and how much better you feel.

- Purchase toys based on the latest research. (You know the videos and books that teach them to appreciate Beethoven and Mozart at six months, and have them fluent in sign language before their first birthday.) Before you know it they will be teaching you the latest technology.
- Boomers are far more educated than our parents were. Participate and volunteer in your grandchildren's pre-schools and schools. Share your expertise with the administration, teachers, or students. Every grandparent has something to contribute, and every school can use their help.

INSIGHTS

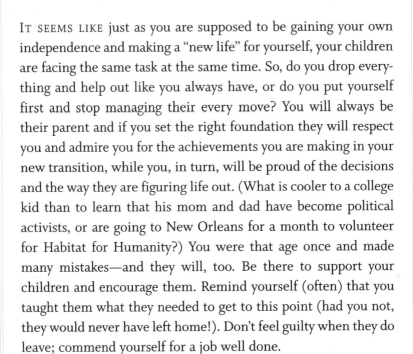

IT SEEMS LIKE just as you are supposed to be gaining your own independence and making a "new life" for yourself, your children are facing the same task at the same time. So, do you drop everything and help out like you always have, or do you put yourself first and stop managing their every move? You will always be their parent and if you set the right foundation they will respect you and admire you for the achievements you are making in your new transition, while you, in turn, will be proud of the decisions and the way they are figuring life out. (What is cooler to a college kid than to learn that his mom and dad have become political activists, or are going to New Orleans for a month to volunteer for Habitat for Humanity?) You were that age once and made many mistakes—and they will, too. Be there to support your children and encourage them. Remind yourself (often) that you taught them what they needed to get to this point (had you not, they would never have left home!). Don't feel guilty when they do leave; commend yourself for a job well done.

Yes, the nest will feel empty and you will also feel empty inside. It is okay to cry, but I have found that it is the adjustment to your new life more than the actual loss of your children that causes the most tears. And if you think back about how you cried the first day they left for kindergarten, you realize that it's not much different now. They were leaving you to make new friends, and to start a new life on their own (or at least between 8 AM and 3:15 PM five days a week). You felt old then, and you probably feel old now. Major life transitions make us feel that way. Remember that our job as parents never ends; you are their anchors and they needed you then and they need you now. Expect those frantic calls asking what to do about a lost credit card (most likely yours, so you better not hang up). As you lay awake all night worried and wondering if your child has stopped crying yet, he or she was "over it" ten minutes after you hung up, and is well onto the next crisis (or college party). And, the next day, when you call to ask about the credit card, don't be surprised if the response is "what credit card?".

Remember not to hover over your children: Mentor, but don't manage them. Let them fly solo and give them and you the opportunity to map out a new life for yourselves. Recognize that it is not our children's responsibility to worry about how we will spend our years once they are out of the house. Don't make them feel guilty about growing up and living their own lives. Whether you are a parent who has raised a child by yourself, or a married couple, it is your time to start over again. Be proactive in meeting some people who have shared interests, and who might even be going through the empty nest period as well. (And of course, try to meet the ones who have had successful transitions—you can learn a lot from them.) There is no shame in starting to live again. If you have held off dealing with your marital problems "until the kids are gone," now is the time to deal with them. If you are single and didn't want to date while the kids were still home, you can start now. (If you have been dating and have hidden your significant other in the closet, no one's home and you can let them out now.)

True, a very wonderful stage of our life is closing. (And you have albums of pictures to prove how wonderful it was.) We may be afraid of being left alone, as we look ahead into our senior years. We find ourselves asking the question "What will we do with ourselves now that the children are gone?" Remember that boredom is really the absence of other feelings. Find creative outlets for yourself. Make a list of all the things you have always said that you wanted to "do someday." Start doing them now. If you need a harsh reality check, title your list *100 Things to Do Before I Die*. Finally, the sheer time, energy, and emotion involved in raising children and working outside the home often leaves parents with a sense of being disconnected from each other as individuals, outside of the family-raising activities. Get connected and get involved. Make a new life for yourself and enjoy it! (Whether or not the kids approve.)

The most important thing I have learned over the years about this subject is that the fear you have of your children leaving is larger than the actual adjustment to them not being home.

In the meantime, it is important to reassess and reevaluate all the important skills you learned at the parenting job and put them to use somewhere else. Join a charitable organization, get involved with a community group, or volunteer to answer the phone at a crisis center (no problem there, you've raised teenagers). Middle age parents find sharing and caring for others a very rewarding and meaningful experience. Yes, your kids will be calling home from college, and you will give them great peace of mind (not to mention be a good role model) if they see you are busy doing something you enjoy, that makes you feel good, and helps others.

Recognize that it is not saying goodbye to your children at the dorm, altar, or the new apartment that is so painful, it is saying goodbye to the only life you have known for the past twenty some-odd years. Once you kiss them goodbye, and after you are finished crying the entire way home, you usually have one more meltdown before you can begin to heal. (And that comes from opening the door to their empty bedroom, which is, as always, a mess—so this time you are screaming, as well as crying.) Crying heals and is a necessary part of goodbye.

YOUR AGING PARENTS

Parenting Your Parents

BACKGROUND

DEALING WITH OUR parents is something that we have done all our lives, and (in theory, at least) we should be pretty good at it by the time we are in our forties. But sometimes it seems as if they only get more difficult as they get older. We fought with them during our teens, they forgave our bad behavior throughout our twenties, and they became our friends as we raised our own children. But now, somehow, the roles have reversed and we find ourselves in midlife trying to forgive them for their unacceptable behavior, or our lousy childhood (that we just realized was entirely their fault). Their demands of our time and for our attention seem unreasonable, and often impossible. As our parents are living longer with more chronic illnesses we are escorting them to more doctors' visits, and spend hours on the phone trying to find someone proficient in translating healthcare benefits into English. We try to gain the support and assistance of siblings and even spouses to help make decisions and coordinate logistics. But that doesn't always help, and you end up sharing your tales of woe with your new best friend (at the Medicare office).

Because your kids have gone, or are at least old enough to stay home alone, you have been "chosen" as senior care manager for your parents, and given the job of social services liaison. Like you need any more jobs.

You long for the days when the biggest decision you had to make was what new appliance to buy for mom or dad's birthday gift. These thoughts go fleeting across your mind, and then you feel guilty. After all, you remember all they did for you growing up, and besides, you really do want to help them. However, your feelings go from sad to mad over the course of any given phone call. One day they are complaining about their leaking roof—but refuse to sell the house and move to a retirement community. The next day you go over to visit only to find your mother or father looking pale with news of bad test results that they just didn't want to worry you with. Sometimes it is hard to believe, but as parents become very old they do give their first priority to their children and grandchildren, and want to see them thrive, even if it means ignoring some of their own needs, or downplaying their own conditions. The juggling act is not easy. Balancing your needs and theirs takes the dedication and patience that you hope your own children will someday have for you when you need their help getting out of the chair, or into the car.

You hated it when your parents told you throughout your life "they knew what was best for you." But now with the tables turned, you, your siblings, and your family think they know what is best for mom and dad. If your parents are still intact, emotionally this is a difficult conversation to have. You ask them what they want and they usually tell you something you don't want to hear, and that you know is not best for them. You ask them if they would like to move to a beautiful retirement home or in with you (or a relative) so that they will be safe and not alone. The answer usually is a resounding NO: They would rather stay where they are and live dangerously. (Life on the edge is very appealing to seniors—what do they have to lose?) Most middle age adults feel exhausted from the fighting and eventually give up and give in to their parents' wishes. While they are home sleeping with the help of Ambien, you are up worrying that they will be okay by morning. (Actually they are just giving you another reason not to go back to sleep after your child calls from college with a crisis of their own. Tell them to all take a number!)

Most children have an image of their parents that remains constant throughout their younger lives. But when you become fifty and they are in their seventies you see them in a different light. They begin to look old to you, and that makes you sad. You begin by noticing the little things: they go to mall with you but wait outside on a bench for you while you shop; they would like to make your dinner together a little earlier because they are afraid to drive at night; or you find them napping after a morning of grocery shopping. Looking at them now as fragile can be heartbreaking. You have lived your entire life depending on your parents for security, advice, and support and now you have become all of those things to them. Suddenly you begin to feel alone, and their mortality becomes very real to you. All the years they joked with you and said, "You should because I won't be around forever" or "Who will ever do this for you when I'm gone" now has real meaning to you. Often we make a pact with ourselves to communicate our love and emotions to our parents, but when we tell them how we are feeling we learn they have not put their hearing aid in to listen. So we say it anyway, because once they are gone we no longer have "home" to go back to and don't want to be left with nothing but regrets.

Symptoms

FEELINGS

- You feel overwhelmed and restless
- You feel burdened and resentful
- You feel increased anxiety about death
- You feel as if you have lost part of your past or part of yourself
- You feel a loss of control
- You feel fatigue, stress, anxiety, and depression
- You feel anxious, afraid, worried, and uptight
- You feel left out of family discussions and decisions
- You feel accountable to your parent and to your siblings
- You feel unappreciated
- You feel embarrassed by your parents' behavior

THOUGHTS

- Thinking your parents' problems and caretaking are your ultimate responsibility

- Believing that you will be blamed by others if you make a wrong healthcare or living arrangement decision
- Realizing your health, sanity, work, hobbies, friends, etc. are being affected adversely
- Thinking your parent is ungrateful and inconsiderate

BEHAVIORS

- Sending messages to parents of what they want to hear, or messages that will not upset them. Not telling the truth.
- Making decisions based on guilt or with inadequate information
- Judging other family members on what they can or cannot contribute
- Making promises that you can't keep
- Ignoring your own needs, which is detrimental to yourself and to the person who needs care
- Placing unrealistic expectations on family members

PRESENTING PROBLEMS

Make It All Worthwhile:
Improving Your Parents' Senior Years

All seniors have the capacity in one way or another to enjoy life, however, they sometimes need help doing so. Attitude—and health—are everything, but with encouragement and the right resources you can help make your aging parents' lives worthwhile and meaningful. The problem is that many of us define what we think is meaningful to us, and try to impose that on our parents. You may think that watching their grandchild play soccer would be very meaningful, and when your parent declines the invitation or opportunity you get angry. But consider it from their perspective: I am sure that seeing their grandchild involved in sports is "lovely," but the bleachers may be hard and the sun too hot. It would be more enjoyable for them to have a lunch or visit with their grandchild somewhere where they are comfortable. Try to think of ways that they can be helpful and feel important in your lives, instead of making them sit on the sidelines. There is a reason that all our storybooks have grandmas baking cookies, they enjoy it and they feel appreciated for doing so.

We are living in a day and age where our elderly parents, for the most part, do not return home to live with their children once they are unable to care for themselves. Instead their children go to great lengths to find the best living facility or arrangement for their parents (don't feel guilty it's okay). However, too often they are forgotten or left out of the family loop. To increase their quality of life and to make sure you stay connected to them:

- Keep them up on the family news. Share with them what is going on with the grandkids, your job or your sister-in-law. If they took an interest then they will still be interested now.
- Let your parents make some decisions for the family. Give them a little power and control. (Two things that they feel they have lost if they no longer are living on their own.) Give them an assignment, or a decision to make, like picking a destination for your next family vacation, or selecting the menu for the next holiday meal. If they are still able to help with the cooking or shopping let them but insist that food have some flavor; remember their taste buds dull with age. Make them feel that they are needed (and you might be surprised at what they come up with).
- Hang around together (as much as either one of you can tolerate). Go with them to activities that you both enjoy. If you were always shopping buddies or sports fans ask them to go along. Granted, you won't be able to visit as

many shops or stay as many innings as you did before; but it will give you time to be together. And if there is something that they especially enjoy, suck it up if you don't like it and go along; afterwards, you can encourage them to go by themselves. (Remember that you did the same things with your kids at one time, as did your parents for you. Like when had no one to go to the dinosaur museum, or the penguin parade with so they went with you.)

- Buy them gifts that will stimulate and challenge their minds, and that you will enjoy playing with them. Puzzles and games are a good start, and work your way up to a computer or an iPod. (Don't go overboard—remember that you probably aren't as "quick" with the latest technology as your own kids, either.) New technology can be intimidating and the plan might backfire; as they become more frustrated with the technology they also may become dependent on you.
- Encourage their involvement in things outside the family too, where they can interact with people their own age, other seniors. After much resistance they will find that they have much in common and maybe won't be so dependent on you. This will also give them something to talk to you (or complain) to you about.

Foster Better Communication with Your Parents

Maybe you have never had an easy time talking to your parents, or maybe all you did together was talk. You may find that now, as your parents are aging, it gets even more difficult to communicate with them (even with the hearing aid turned on). It seems like they don't want to listen to you, or they don't want to hear a thing you are saying. But now is the time to talk, listen, laugh, and learn. As frustrating as it is (and that is an understatement for many) try talking things out now, and communicate your thoughts and feelings. You may soon not have a chance to share. Do it for their sake as well as for yours.

You are probably frustrated that after all these years there are certain things that your parents just never "got." Maybe they never understood why you married the woman (or man) who already had a two-year-old of her own; or why you became an accountant instead of a doctor. You may even feel uncomfortable talking to them about their wishes, the future, how much you will miss them when they are gone. There will be things that if left unsaid will haunt you after your parents are gone. As difficult as it may be, talk to them now. Open the dialogue with some of these sentences:

- I always loved the time we spent when I was young doing _____ , or going_____, or when we _____.
- I often regret that we never talked about _____; but maybe this a good time to talk about it.
- I have always felt very close to you when _____.
- I always wished that we could go back and make up for _____.
- I think that I know where you want to _____ (live when you can't live on your own; or what your wishes are as far as end of life care; or where you want to buried). But if I'm wrong tell me and we can talk about it.
- I know we never agreed on _____; but this is something that I think we just carried on from when I was a kid. Maybe now we can talk about it, without being hurtful.
- After years of thinking about _____, and feeling bad about _____; or how much we disagreed or argued about _____ , I realize that that was just part of my _____ (personality, or theirs; or your generation etc.).
- I really need to say I am sorry about _____, or that _____.

Try This

So Conflicted

Identify any conflicts areas—ask yourself:

- **To what extent do I have conflicts with my parents?**
- **What are the areas of conflicts? Are they "carry-overs" from childhood or early adulthood?**

- Are these conflicts caused by my parents' temperaments, my personality, or some combination of both?
- How have I contributed to each conflict?

Who Ever Said That Is What They Wanted?: Determine What Your Parent Truly Wants

You probably have had a lot of intense conversations with your parents over the years. The one about the boyfriend you wanted to marry and that they hated, or the one where you had to tell them that your husband lost his job, or one of your kids needed surgery. But everyone wants to avoid the conversation about his or her wishes regarding healthcare—their wills, and burials—because neither you nor they really even want to think about these things, let alone discuss them. Although your parents openly talk about their health and share more intimate details about their bodies than you may care to hear about, why is this one so hard? Because it is sad for both you and your parents to think that there will be a time that they will have to rely on you, or someone else to take care of them. They have pride and don't want to think of themselves like the people they see on television commercials chasing their grandchildren in motorized carts, or clapping their hands to turn on lights.

You, on the other hand, realize you will be the one responsible for arranging for care, and making the decisions when they are no longer able to do so, so you do need to know. Don't be surprised when you approach the subject if you are met with sarcasm (*You want to kick us out of our home so you can sell it and buy a new car*), resistance (*We have plenty of time to discuss this, now is not the time*), or with denial (*There is no reason to have this discussion, I am perfectly healthy*). Don't push and insist: just wait and try again soon.

PEACE TALKS—DON'T MAKE IT A PLAN OF ATTACK

You are entering into enemy territory when you approach the area of your parents' inability to live alone. Expect to be met with much resistance. This is one battle that can be difficult to win. Just as they have told us growing up to "choose your battles wisely" this is one of them (believe me!).

- Create a game plan strategy and choose the right team players (siblings, friends, the family doctor or physician, whoever knows your parent, someone your parent trusts).
- Choose a good time to begin the talks. Remember timing can be everything. Try not to have this discussion on the way home from your parent's emergency room visit.
- Cover one base at a time. Don't bring up selling the house, moving to assisted living, and the will all at once.
- If you strike out; just try again. The game is far from over.

Listen Up!

If you calm down and learn to listen you may be able to really hear what your parents are trying to tell you without having to make them shout. One of the best skills you can develop is listening. Sometimes it may be difficult to listen, especially if we believe that we know better. But out of respect and dignity for our aging parents, let's assume they can speak for themselves. Most aging seniors really do know what they want and what's best for them, and your parents are no different.

DOES ANYONE HEAR WHAT I AM SAYING!

Assess your own listening skills. Are you guilty of:

1. ____ Daydreaming
2. ____ Discounting information
3. ____ Jumping to conclusions
4. ____ Interrupting
5. ____ Ignoring
6. ____ Losing eye contact

7. ____ Finishing the speaker's thoughts

8. ____ Changing subjects

9. ____ Excessive physical activity

10. ____ Habitually challenging or defying the speaker

If you want to hear what your parents are telling you, practice (you need all the help you get):

1. ____ Paying attention

2. ____ Separating content from personality

3. ____ Being nonjudgmental

4. ____ Being courteous—not interrupting or finishing thoughts and sentences

5. ____ Maintaining natural, comfortable eye contact

6. ____ Asking questions

7. ____ Seeking clarification

8. ____ Sharing your own personal information

9. ____ Reaching agreement or understanding

10. ____ Retaining information over time

Team Work: Working Effectively with Your Siblings to Help Your Parents

Like it or not, the one thing you will always have to share with your siblings is your parents. We might not have liked it when we were younger, and sometimes as adults it can seem just as difficult. As each of us grow up and create our own lives, our own nuclear families become the focus of our world. However, siblings who are not close to one another stay connected at some level through a shared concern for (or obligation to) their parents. In families where siblings don't get along, there may be disagreement in the plans or attention given to parents as they age. If a parent is closer to one sibling than another (or as we the children perceive it, have chosen favorites) sibling rivalry will continue and we might respond differently to accepting responsibility for an aging parent.

Finances, geographical locations, and other factors have an impact on who takes what responsibility. It seems like in every family there is that one child who writes out the checks to help out, or who manages the money that mom and dad have—and there is the other child who lives nearby, or is free to help with the daily logistics of caretaking like driving them to the doctor's office. But, often, as a result of differing attitudes and the stress involved in dealing with aging parents, siblings who were once close find their relationship strained. In other cases siblings who were never close, or who have had past grievances, find themselves coming together to support one another and their parents during these last years. Aging parents want and need their children to be involved in their senior years. If you are an only child, your job is a little tougher in some ways. You have a lot more to do; however, you do not have the stress of negotiating or compromising decisions (as they are usually all yours).

NOT A TIME FOR SIBLING RIVALRY, BUT A GOOD TIME TO ASK QUESTIONS

The most widespread means of taking care of parents is by sharing the responsibility between siblings. No matter what caretaking job you were given, or agreed to take, always try to be sensitive to the primary caregiver. Even if there are several siblings, the caregiving responsibilities are usually not equally shared, and one adult child will emerge as a primary caregiver. If you are not the primary caregiver, maintain some sensitivity toward the one who handles most of the responsibility and do whatever you can to pitch in and help.

- Ask yourself how well this arrangement will work for you and your family.
- Who was "the strong sibling," "the favorite one," and so forth, when you grew up? Which one was I growing up? Do we all still play these roles and assume the same responsibilities we did then? If we don't, what changed?
- What kind of relationship do you and your siblings have today? Is it different than when you grew up? If it is, what happened to change it? Does it have something to do with your parents?
- How well do you get along with your siblings' spouses or significant others; with their children? Of them, who can you depend on to help with your parents?

- How frequently do you and your siblings maintain contact through visits, telephone, and e-mail? Are you happy with the relationship the way it is now? Or would you like it to be different?
- Have you and your brothers and sisters and the whole family grown closer or further apart with age? If so, what do you think it would take to bring them closer together again?

Siblings may not always get along but dealing with aging parents makes them come together—like it or not. This is a time when poor relationships can get better; but sadly it can also cause close relationships to fall apart. If relationships are poor, a parent's illness, need for relocation, or death can create greater distance between siblings. Sometimes siblings compete to do the most for the aged parent, quarrel over care arrangements, accuse each other of negligence, avoid responsibility, and fight for the title of favorite.

Taking Care of Yourself: Balancing Your Parents' Needs and Your Own

At midlife you are most likely just adapting to new routines as the kids are getting older or have fled the nest. Gradually you find that there are more phone calls from mom or dad (usually complaining about each other—or if they live alone, complaining about their health or their neighbor's dog). Your conversations seem to end up with some sort of promise or commitment—and now you are obligated to find the time for one more thing on your calendar. You end up revising your work schedule, changing your social plans, or regretfully having to say "no" to your kids or spouse because grandma or grandpa needs help. Chronically fatigued, and even a little resentful, you manage to keep going. Remember that although the kids may not be happy, or your spouse or boss may not be thrilled, you will have to live with yourself for years after your parents are gone.

This emotional and physical drain affects us and our families at many levels. Our internal resources become tapped and we find ourselves with little patience, and little energy. Many of us find that we may have to help out financially, as our aging parents have not prepared for their retirement;

sadly the choice comes down to them moving in with you, or you helping find someplace for them to live where they can get the help they need. (There's no escape: there's guilt on either side.) Perhaps it is fine with you to have a parent come live with you, but it is not so fine with your spouse. Already the fighting has begun, and your parent is still living on his or her own. Remember to ask for help when you can and look for compromises with each other. It is easy to be so wrapped up in providing care for your parents that you ignore your own well-being. (If this sounds familiar, it is: we discussed the same thing earlier in Session 8, regarding our own kids.)

The stress related to the caregiving role depends on many things; try to assess how these things affect YOUR life:

- Where do your parents want to live? In what kind of facility? (*Their answer may be your guest bedroom, be prepared with an answer before the discussion.*)
- How well do you get along with you parent? How obligated or guilty do you feel about providing your time and energy to the caregiving of parent? (*Honestly, we have some guilt.*)
- How will your new responsibilities affect your spouse? How do they feel about your parents, their in-laws? (*Be clear on this one because you want your spouse to be around many more years after your parents are gone.*)
- How disruptive will this be to your day-to-day living? (*Take a look at your datebook before you answer that.*)
- Who else is going to help you out here? Or are you doing this on your own? (*Once you accept the assignment it becomes your job alone if no one else has signed up.*) Enlist all the help you can get.

When making the decision whether or not to provide care, and how much to provide, consider your readiness and that of your family, to take on this role. Evaluate both the positive and negative aspects. Taking on the role of caregiver may mean having to make changes in your social life and work schedules, stretching time and money, chronic fatigue, uncertainty of what the future holds, and extra strain on you, your family, and those you come in contact with. Your family's lifestyle and your own will change. It may mean less time to spend with your spouse or children;

revised work and home schedules; increased emotional and physical stress which could result in a weight gain or loss; depression; and problems managing family, work, or social engagements. Taking on the role of caregiver is not an easy one. Adjustments, time, and understanding are a must.

Despite the number of changes and adjustments, the benefits can be numerous to the caregiver. Caregivers cite the following benefits they reap:

- Enhanced sense of self-worth
- A chance to improve relations with the parent
- Reassurance that the parent is getting optimal care
- Satisfaction of living in accordance with one's religious and/or ethical beliefs or principles
- Greater sense of purpose and meaning
- Feeling that one has coped successfully with a potentially difficult life situation
- Satisfaction of repaying the parent for what they've done for you in the past
- An opportunity to make up for missed time together
- Feeling closer to the parent as a result of helping
- Increased patience and endurance
- A better perspective and understanding of their own aging

Just Calm Down: Coping With Caregiver Burnout and Stress

Caregiver burnout is a state of physical, emotional, and mental exhaustion, and often, a caregiver (even when we are caring for our own parent) can become pessimistic and unconcerned. Burnout occurs when caregivers don't seek needed help, believing that we can do it alone (or have no other choice). Caregivers who are "burned out" may experience fatigue, stress, anxiety, and depression. Compounding this is the fact that we often feel guilty when we spend time on ourselves rather than on our parent—taking a break becomes a selfish act (*This is wrong, of course. Quite the opposite is true. You are doing your parent and you a favor.*)

Remember that you still have kids, a spouse, and probably a boss that needs you, too. Unless you preserve yourself and avoid burnout, no one will benefit from your good intentions. Enlist help and make a plan.

BE PROACTIVE

- **Identify the emergency exit.** Give everyone the chance to speak their mind before it becomes a crisis situation so you are all in agreement on what to do in the event of your parent's emergency.
- **Make a relief plan.** Decide just how much time everyone can afford to help. Try to schedule as many things time ahead of time that you can (surgeries, doctor's appointments, and haircuts, etc.).
- **Choose a speaker for the house.** Someone needs to be the one to responsible for speaking to the doctors, Medicare, or living facility offices when necessary. (*Choose the person with the most patience they will need it!*) If too many people are involved, things become more complicated and miscommunication can occur.
- **Get it in writing.** Be clear regarding your parent's wishes are in the event they are not able to tell you. Have their wishes written down somewhere. This will help avoid legal and family arguments—maybe. Be prepared in case what they wanted is not an option when the time comes to make a decision. (*In that case, just do the best you can.*)
- **Be honest with yourself.** Be realistic as to what you can and cannot to do to help with your parents' caregiving. Don't make promises you can't keep. You can always change your mind later if you want to give more, but having to cut back later on puts a strain on everyone. Of course circumstances change, and if they do everyone will understand. (Just don't call at the last minute and tell the night nurse she has to work another shift because your hair salon just changed your appointment to 7 PM.)

ASK FOR HELP AND DON'T FORGET THE PRACTICAL THINGS

Try not to let the potential for stress overwhelm you: Share responsibilities and share family problems with friends, and/or professionals (who can be a great resource). Remember that asking others is a sign of courage—to do what is best for your family—not weakness.

Realize that many of your friends and family are willing to help—don't be shy in asking, and don't reject their offers of assistance because you believe that the caregiving responsibility is only your concern.

There are so many major concerns—health issues, wills, doctor's visits—that it can be easy to neglect day-to-day concerns. Who handles hands-on care, housekeeping, and transportation? What about laundry, taking care of the yard, and grocery shopping? How do we arrange and monitor these things if we don't live nearby? These are all things, to consider now as your parent ages. (*Buy yourself a good weekly planner—you'll need it!*)

TAKE A PREVENTATIVE APPROACH

Always strive to help parents find a way to stay involved with life, and to learn and grow to meet their own needs. Motivate them by giving emotional support and inspiration. Encourage them to have hopes, dreams, ambitions, and new goals—and then provide backup as they reach for those goals, whether through arranging or encouraging new relationships, or rekindling old friendships. If your parents are in poor health, do everything you can to make sure that they keep in touch with others. Bring stimulation from the outside world to ill parents by providing books, magazines, and conversation—or rent a movie together. Don't just drop them off at home or put them to bed. Discuss the movie, talk to them about the magazine. It will keep their minds sharp. The goal here is to prolong independence, instill confidence, and actually prolong physical health.

GREAT EXPECTATIONS

You may feel responsible for all of your parents' care, and you may become frustrated or overwhelmed. It is normal when we feel that we are responsible for every last component of our parents' care—within reason. Sometimes we become so consumed in our role of caretaker that we neglect our other roles. You are still their adult daughter or son and can only do so much. Don't place undue burdens upon yourself. Stop thinking that your parents' care is your ultimate responsibility, and the quality of their lives is solely dependent on you. As with everything else we have done for our children and families for the past thirty or so years, we do what we thought was right and hope for the best.

Manage Your Stress

Learn to recognize when you are feeling stressed. (*When your stomach aches and you are pulling your hair out of your head, for example.*) Then, choose a way to deal with your stress. When caring for an elderly parent you can't always eliminate the event or things that lead to your stress, but you can change how you react to stress, which is often the best, and the most practical way.

- Relax a little. Don't worry about things you can't control. (*e.g., the long wait in the emergency room.*)
- Get ready to go. Prepare to the best of your ability for events you know may be stressful. (*e.g., escorting your parent to the Medicaid Office. Rest up the night before and bring a book.*)
- Don't fight it. Work to resolve conflicts with other people. (*e.g., differing opinions with relatives regarding your parent's healthcare arrangements.*)
- Maintain your balance. Set realistic goals at home and at work. (*e.g., use time management skills to help create a schedule for you to balance all your demands.*)

You Can't Go Home Anymore: Grieving the Death of a Parent

At any age, losing a parent is one of the deepest losses anyone experiences. Throughout our childrearing years we stay busy, and our parents are young enough and usually active in their own lives. Then they get older, and need us more; our kids are grown and there we are back together, entangled in each other's lives—whether we really want to be or not. We get close again, argue like we did when we were teenagers (only this time around you are the one holding the keys to the car), and then they pass away either suddenly or over a period of time. The cycle is similar to when your children first became teens and became impossible to deal with: You couldn't wait for them to move out and offered to help pack their suitcases many times. Then, during their senior year they became sweet, mature, and you became close friends again, and then they, too, left. In both cases you felt abandoned and alone. Even as an adult, when your parent dies you have lost that most secure place in your heart, and a piece of you also dies.

You may feel increased anxiety fearing that you are the next generation to die, and perhaps you will experience the same sort of death. The sudden death of a parent gives us no time to prepare or say all the things you should have said, and regrets can run rampant. All of a sudden your life is turned upside-down, especially if caring for them was part of your daily routine. Parents have the most special and influential force in a child's life. Even an as an adult you still are "their" child. The meaning of losing a parent is different for everyone, and largely depends on the importance of the parent/child relationship that has existed in the past.

If your parent has been suffering with a terminal illness, the relief that death provides is better than them suffering needlessly. But while it can certainly be better for them, it may not help you emotionally. Your sense of relief brings feelings of guilt. After so many months or years of emotional preoccupation most likely you are ready to get on with your life, and think that staying busy or making changes will ease the pain. Take time to grieve, and focus on yourself and your loss. Everything else can wait.

When a parent dies, those around us may say things like, "he had a good life," or "you're lucky that you had them for as long as you did," doing their best to comfort us. But in reality there is nothing to say, because nothing will bring our parents back. And likewise, there is not much for us to do, except to flounder for a time—because no matter our age—we will always be our parents' children. Nothing can ever replace them, because from day one, they have been our teacher, guide, and unconditional source of love. (At least we hope so.) One of the worst things about losing a parent, especially if the relationship has been strained, is coming to terms with what "might have been." Death's finality takes away any chance to mend the relationship: Besides all the grief, there is now the additional pain of guilt and regret.

INSIGHTS

No matter how old you are you will always be your parent's child. Even as an adult you will look to your parents for security and love. When they age, and the roles become in some way reversed, the adjustments you have to make can be difficult and physically and emotionally draining. The images you have of your parents' youth and vitality can become shattered as they become frail and older. You look at old photos of when they were young and can't believe how fast the time has gone. This may the first time you begin to feel some regrets. When you have to repeat yourself because they can't hear you, or you notice their skin getting wrinkled, you don't want to admit that this is your parent. Your siblings call with similar observations; and one day, when everyone is agreement that "something must be done about mom and dad" the reality sets in. Your roles slowly reverse and you become the caretaker. Frustration, hopelessness (and sometimes even anger and resentment) set in: Just as you have entered midlife and are free from all those childrearing obligations, you have to deal with this. (And of course, even thinking these things brings additional guilt.) However, it is okay to feel all of these things because everyone does, and they are natural. Try to reevaluate everything and look at what you're facing through a different perspective.

As a parent or a spouse you have had to make adjustments your whole life. You are used to caring for the people you love. So really, why is this any different? You didn't throw your teenager out of the house for driving you crazy (although I am sure you may have considered it), so why would you would you abandon your parent when they need you most? Being exhausted, overwhelmed, and overworked is nothing new. But let's face it: At midlife you are not as young as you used to be. So asking for help becomes essential. This is not a time when being a martyr will win you any awards—ask for some help. And as for your parents, I know that they all say they can't hear what you are saying (especially when you have something important to say) but try to communicate with them. Have them turn up the hearing aid—and be sure to open your ears—to find out what they are saying. It will make life easier if you know what their wishes are.

At middle age your life is not near being over. So don't stop living your own life to accommodate your parent's life. Find balance and set boundaries. Limit your trips to the grocery store. If they run out of tomatoes before the next trip, tell them to eat cucumbers instead. Develop empathy in tackling those moments of trouble. It will help you deal with them more effectively. Yes, they can be demanding and even mean—but try to put yourself in their place and try to imagine how you will feel given the same set of circumstances (and yes, your own time will come one day). Come on, we have all eaten some of the no-salt, no-fat, no-flavor food that make up many senior menu plans. Wouldn't you be complaining?

Remember they are not the same people that raised you, so don't treat them as you did when they were your age. Look at them as they are now; remember them as you did when you were a child. When they are gone you will want to be proud of all they have done for you, and proud of all that you gave back to them. Have no regrets. Feel lucky if your parents are still around to share in your midlife years. It is gift to be treasured by you and your children.

Understand that your aging parent may not always be kind, patient, or considerate with you, as the frustrating parts of aging get the better of them. A sympathetic attitude toward old age will facilitate tackling those moments of trouble and help you deal with them more effectively. The important thing is that your parents feel they belong, and do not become isolated. Okay, I can hear it now—you have tried this, and they just "refuse to go," and I believe you. Don't stop trying. You may hit on the one thing that interests them. If seniors do not use their brains actively they will quickly fall short in their cognitive abilities. Music, games, books, and magazines can help pass the time and keep their minds sharp.

Losing a parent is one of the most profound losses we will experience. The sudden death of a parent gives us no time to prepare or say all the things you should have said, and regrets can run rampant. All of a sudden your life is turned upside-down, especially if caring for them was part of your daily routine. Even an as an adult you still are "their" child. The meaning of losing a parent is different for everyone, and largely depends on the importance of the parent/child relationship that existed in the past.

When your parent dies you become "the next generation," you become their legacy. This is why it is important to involve your children and your grandchildren in their lives. They are the link that will carry the spirit, tradition, and heritage on. Your children have limited time to gain wisdom from them, and the stronger the connection that develops between the grandparents and grandchildren, the stronger bond your family will have for generations to come. Also, by devoting time and offering love and support to your parents during their final years of life, you will be creating a wonderful example of kindness, compassion, and caring for your own children. Remember: How you treat your parents during this last phase of their life will be the role model your children will follow when your time comes and you need their help and want them to be close.

ESPECIALLY FOR MIDLIFE MEN

It's a Guy Thing

BACKGROUND

MEN NEVER FEEL that anything is a crisis, unless it has to do with the stock market crashing or their favorite team not making it to the play-offs. Although everyone else around them notices that at midlife men begin to act a little confused, look a little lost, and appear somewhat restless—men look in the mirror and only notice a few bald spots, and some gray chest hairs. If they have a wife, kids, and a good job they consider themselves a successful family man—until now, at midlife, when they start to question what success really means. They once believed in marriage, work, and friendship but now none of it really seems that important or that great. After years of following the same routine, having sex with the same woman, reporting to the same boss, and listening to the same friends complain, they begin to question everything that they once believed in. Nights of insomnia, days of fatigue, and moments of despair may become the norm. Yet, most men believe that like everything else, this too will pass.

But then the moment comes when men feel they must act on these feelings of despair, and get out of the rut. They start to regret roads not taken. (Why didn't they drop out of college and sail around the world with that hot girl who was so in love with them?) They dread that the second half of life will hold no more surprises. They begin to feel a sharp longing for something or someone new, whether it's a new thirty-foot boat or the cocktail waitress who asks if there is anything else they need. Men in crisis often obsess about big questions. (*Does my life matter? Does my wife matter?*) And it is often the jolt of some bad news—a friend has a heart attack, or the wife packs her bags—that wakes them right up, fast. Meanwhile, men that have never married think in reverse: They question why they didn't marry their high school sweetheart and have lots of babies. What were they thinking when they chose to spend half of their lives in relationships with gorgeous women who meant nothing to them—only to find that now at midlife, they are alone and can't even find one halfway decent-looking girl who really wants them? Men aren't blind. They can see the extra few pounds they have put on, even if they're squinting at the small print on the menu pages. All of a sudden their wives look better to them, and they begin to long for the intimate relationship they once had with them. After soul-searching (and perhaps losing a job, wife, or family) men often want to emerge from midlife as better men. They want to live more meaningful lives and make up for lost years. Whether you are one of those men—or you are a woman reading this hoping to better understand the man in your life—this section will help you understand some of what midlife men are going through.

Symptoms

FEELINGS

- You feel trapped in your marriage, or in your job
- You feel disappointment and resentment about mistakes you have made
- You feel remorse and regrets about roads not taken
- You feel dread that life holds no more surprises
- You feel bored and discontented with everything
- You feel afraid of getting old and being alone
- You feel inadequate as a husband, or as a lover
- You feel fear and confusion and worry that you have to pull away from or destroy the old in order to move on to something new

- You are feeling anxious about the future, or maybe you are just generally anxious and don't know exactly why
- You feel a little depressed, or maybe you have had a bout of clinical depression
- You feel that you are more irritable and more emotional in general

THOUGHTS

- Your life isn't as much fun as it used to be
- You question the value of what you do for a living
- You are thinking about retiring; but are not sure if you will like it
- You are remembering what life was like when you were younger
- You need a change because you are bored with the same routine
- You question things in which you once believed, like marriage, work, and friendships

BEHAVIORS

- You can't seem to make decisions as easily as you used to, and you have lost some confidence in your abilities
- Your roles as a son, a father, a husband, or a friend begin to change
- You try to spend more time with your wife and family
- You become involved in managing your aging parents' healthcare and daily living
- You resist the idea of your wife's new freedom
- You find yourself involved in dangerous or risky activities
- You begin to flirt with women; or you have an affair
- You decide to quit your job; or sell your business
- You become impulsive and irresponsible

Physical

- You notice some gray hair, or wrinkles
- You are taking longer to recover from injuries and illness

- You've noticed you don't have as much physical stamina as you used to have
- You've put on a few pounds, and are feeling a little overweight
- You've had to get reading glasses to make out the small print— and now all print looks smaller
- You are not as interested in sex as you used to be, or you have experienced some changes in your sexuality that are worrying you
- Sex with your partner isn't as exciting as it used to be
- You find yourself daydreaming about having sex with other women, and are maybe masturbating more and finding it more satisfying because you don't have to worry about not performing well
- You are having some problems in your marriage, or maybe you have recently been separated or divorced
- You feel as though you are dead inside, and that the zest in your life is gone

PRESENTING PROBLEMS

Not So Interested: A Decreased Desire for Sex—And Just About Everything Else

Most middle age men watch Viagra commercials and privately think, "Yep, that's me. I can identify with that guy." (And of course they secretly hope that their wives will respond like, or be as beautiful as, that woman in the commercial.) Men can ignore many of the physical changes that occur in middle age: running a little slower around the track, the aches and pains after a tennis match, or some fatigue after a Saturday filled with errands. But they can't ignore the changes in their sexuality. Many middle age men report feeling a decrease in sexual desire, they begin to question their performance, and find that sex is just not as exciting as it used to be. So, along with questioning everything else in life, they ask, "What kind of man am I?"

It is not just sex that men lose the vitality for: it's everything. The things they once liked to do and enjoy just don't mean as much these days. Hanging out with the guys on Friday nights becomes boring. The vacation to Bermuda becomes just alright—which is starting to sound a little like depression. This is a good time to talk to the ones you love about how you are feeling. Don't make everyone guess. Men aren't used to discussing their feelings, and have been criticized by their wives for years for not opening up to them. Most men will argue that talking about feelings won't change the way they feel about something and doesn't solve a problem—a problem is still a problem whether you talk about it or not. But talking about how you feel does help. Expressing how you feel will make you feel better because the people around you that love you will help you through this time. The fact is that you are changing. Your life is changing. So changing how you look at things can help. And once you open up the door for communication, the potential for a stronger relationship will be realized. After years of "ignoring one another" while raising the kids you need to get to know each other as the new people you are today. Through communication and mutual sharing, you will be well on your way to enriching and strengthening your marriage.

Maybe you have been having problems in your marriage for years, and wanted to wait until the kids were older or gone to deal with them. Now is the time. You have invested a lot of years in the family, and have a lot more years together. So why not try to make those years better? Even if you haven't experienced problems, midlife is the start of a new stage for you both. Be sure that you communicate and have realistic expectations—and don't ever assume that you know what your spouse is feeling or thinking. Ask questions to clarify each other's position on issues before decisions are made. Each partner has an obligation to verbalize his or her own expectations to avoid misunderstandings. Show your appreciation and affection for one another. Sometimes partners who have been married a long time unknowingly take each other for granted and expressions of how to show your appreciation can be forgotten. Showing appreciation and affection are powerful methods of strengthening a marriage. Love must be shown in words *and* actions. Most importantly, make the commitment to grow with one another and together for the second half of your marriage. Let go of disappointments in each other and look forward to the second half of married life, making it the best it can be!

Does My Life Matter?: As a Matter of Fact, It Does

Middle-aged men have missed out on a lot throughout the years, and at this stage in their lives are now beginning to realize it. They have worked hard to provide for themselves, and for their families. They think that no one listens to them. Mom has been around more and knows what she is doing, and the younger kid at work seems to have all the bright ideas. In midlife men begin to slow down, and make an effort to reconnect, and regain those things they feel they have lost. However, when they do, they can be faced with resentment from their families, who ask, "Where have you been all these years?" Their kids are growing up and leaving for college, or moving out, or getting married and there is the feeling that there is no time left to make it up. Midlife is a time to sit back and think of your accomplishments and your failures, and attempt to repeat the things you did right, and learn from your mistakes. Your life does matter, and midlife is the time you can make it matter to more people. You may feel like your opinion doesn't matter and no one really cares, but that is because you have lost the confidence and self-worth you had when you were younger.

WHY DOES IT MATTER?

Looking hard at where you have been all these years will help you figure out where you want to go on the next journey in life. It is not so much what you think about life right now, as it is what you think about *you* right now. Fill in the blanks below:

- You achieved great success in business, marriage, family, and _____.
- You need to work harder at accomplishing _____.
- You've always been able to enjoy _____.
- You need to start enjoying something new like _____ or _____again.
- _____ was the best change you ever made in your life.
- You need to change _____, staring now.
- You always felt marriage was all about _____.

- You've learned that is more about _____.
- You always wanted a family that would _____.
- You now hope your family will _____.
- You have always lived your life believing that happiness comes from _____.
- Now you believe that it comes from _____.

Where Is My Motorcyle?: Unfulfilled Dreams

Most men didn't grow up idealizing work and hoping that someday they would be able to "do a man's job." They were men and knew that they would have a "man's job" someday (be a fireman, an engineer, an airplane pilot). However, they often were pressured into going into the same careers and lifestyles as their parents, and in the process robbed themselves of their dreams. When we are young we put on a public face that helps us cope, and get along, and achieve what is expected of us. But behind that mask, we hide all of our fear, pain, and neuroses, along with all the other things we don't want the world to see. Later in life, the stress of an unfulfilling life can result in poor diets, excess alcohol consumption or drug use, work stress, and dysfunctional relationships. But most men still fail to change their ways or seek help. Research has found that men's "dream fulfillment" goes downhill from their mid-30s onward, whereas women (who normally put their dreams on hold in their 20s for childrearing) more often report that they have fulfilled a dream during their midlife years.

It is also common for middle-aged men to find it difficult to discuss their emotional issues, have few friends outside work, and possess limited coping strategies. While some men experience a loss of meaning, a sense of isolation, and loneliness about work, marriage, and sexual satisfaction, others attempt to redefine their sense of identity by revisiting their youth. It is not until midlife that we take off the mask and really look outside of ourselves and look at our lives. Since men typically derive a large sense of their ego from their jobs, if they are unhappy in life and with themselves, it is usually a clue that their employment is unsatisfactory. The prospect of never being able to have that dream job leads to the realization that they may never have that dream life, either. Midlife is a time to create new dreams for the future.

Shifting Gears:
Difficulty Coping with Changing Marital Roles

Marriages are usually at their lowest point at midlife (no surprise if you have some idea of all of the changes going on). Although men and women have tried to equalize (in some cases) their roles, they have usually fallen into some type of role routine, accompanied by some sort of role "rules" (he manages the finances, she disciplines the kids). At middle age no one has to pretend they are happy with their assignments, because no one is around anymore to pass judgment. Some women become more willing to take risks as they grow less concerned about what others think. Men typically have never worried about pretense—and if they did it was one of independence and dominance. Women typically have submerged their identity when their children were younger, to appear as a nurturing, stable role model for their offspring (*or at least tried*). Once the children are grown, many midlife women feel a sense of liberation, and will shed their pretenses. The problems arise when the men they live with come home to someone new, and to new rules. The game has changed and many men don't like it; and there is no changing the channel. That is not to say they don't still love their wives. (Hey, you used to boast to your friends about how brainy she was, right? Don't blame her if she's finally using it now.) Great: so you've "lost" your kids, your parents won't be around much longer, and now your wife is leaving to find Nirvana. Just consider it another form of adjustment you have to deal with.

Some women find midlife so liberating that they make changes that are often perceived by their mates as selfish, unfair, and inconsiderate. (Sounds like things they have accused you of over the years. But wasn't eighteen holes of golf a little "selfish" when your wife was home preparing dinner for your boss?) Remember that women are not complaining about the choices they have made over the years, it's just that now they are celebrating the opportunity to act more independently, and be free to be themselves. Middle-aged men need to get to know the "new woman" who has emerged. After all, this is the perfect chance to "have that other woman" they may or may not have been daydreaming about.

Wish I Was Young Again: Health Risks and Midlife Burnout

Men in midlife have a significantly increased risk of heart disease, work related stress, obesity, alcohol addiction, and depression and suicide. Research indicates that men are aware of the health risks of these diseases yet they fail to change their behavior or seek help. (Surprised?) As a result, men remain emotionally isolated and stressed, contributing to poor health and an increased risk for a life threatening disease. In an attempt to regain their sense of identity men choose to revisit their youth instead of enlisting the help of their spouses, friends, and professionals.

If you've ever noticed yourself thinking things like, "I'm tired of it all" or "I just want to get out of here," you're one of the many men who may be experiencing midlife burnout. Understanding the reasons we get burned out will help you make the right life decisions, and reduce the stress you are feeling.

Midlife Burnout Checklist
Can you relate? Does this sound like something you would say?

1. _____ I'm ready to snap: We are not as young as we used to be; and we are not as good at handling stress as we used to be. The recovery time for a midlife person is slower; and missed sleep adds to our inability to battle the effects of stress. With all the changes going on at midlife you may find yourself stressed out and over the edge. (*And no, a martini or cigarette is not the answer.*)

2. _____ I don't think I like my job: You spend years in your twenties and thirties trying to be happy and successful at your career. Your job becomes a priority in life, and usually is rewarding. After all those years at the same job many men reach midlife and begin to find their careers unfulfilling. (*But*

then again they seem to find everything unfulfilling so just add it to list, right?)

3. _____ I have got to shift gears: The big question when you were younger was "What kind of wife, and what kind of life will make me happy?" And if we didn't ask ourselves that, everyone else asked us. Now, men at midlife find themselves asking different question: "Why didn't I think harder about what I wanted when I was twenty five?" Or they ask "How did I end up here, at this stage in my life?"

4. _____ I'm feeling low: As a midlife man, you may have made the fortune you banked on and have the house, the car, and all the technology toys you ever wanted; but you may also feel a large degree of insecurity, and feel that you are not worth very much. You have slowed down, and after you are done playing you start to wonder; "Is that all there is?" Suddenly you feel that life is about more than fun and games but you don't what. (*But you still keep the toys, right?*)

INSIGHTS

MIDLIFE IS FAR more than a handful of physical changes. It often brings a reordering of priorities, a change in values, deep soul-searching about the meaning of life, the facing of our own mortality, and a loss of social power, status, and position.

Sure, no man wants to go through midlife or old age alone; but most are so unhappy with their lives that they might as well be alone. For many the dreams they carried with them never materialized, and they feel it is too late to start over, so why should they bother? Their families have grown up and moved on, and they have missed out on their best years. As men face their own mortality, they begin to reprioritize their lives. And one of the first priorities seems to be to return and relive parts of their youth. Just when women think men should be moving forward with their lives, they start to regress, and begin to act childish. (Actually, you just got all the kids out of the house—and who needs another baby to care of?) For men, this is just part of growing up that they didn't get to do as children, and need to do before they can find peace in this next stage of life.

So much has changed while you were sleeping for the last twenty years. Men wake up one day and wonder who that woman is next to him. Women don't recognize this agitated and unhappy man as the same person they married. After many years of so little real conversation, so little intimacy—and with the kids around all the time, so little sex—you are out of practice with how to really talk to one another. Sure you have spent hours "discussing" (not talking about) your children. But those were just exercises in information exchange. Now that you have no one to interrupt you at the dinner table, or on the phone, it is time to listen to what is really being said (including your feelings, values, and fears). Try to listen with your heart and not your brain. (Hey I am sure you got the "silent treatment" enough times over the years to have developed that skill.) You know you are feeling differently, and everyone else knows it, too. As a man, you need to start talking about what is going on. If you had been having troubles at work, trust me, you would be spilling every detail *(over and over and over again)*. But when it comes to admitting that you are getting old, and are feeling scared, you don't say a word. Your relationships have weathered worse storms than this. It is so important to remember that—and take care of yourself, and of each other.

Men, in particular, don't like their feelings being probed, or being demanded to explain themselves. Actually, no one really does, so try not to ask "why" questions of your partner—they create an immediate defensiveness—and people at midlife generally don't know "why" we are doing things. (*Why didn't I get the promotion I deserved? Why won't my mother give in and move to the retirement center? Why does my wife insist that we let our twenty-five-year-old daughter come live with us?)* Why is midlife so hard? Because life as you knew it has changed. You are struggling, and want support. It is okay to ask for help. Men want to return home to their families that they have missed, and make up for lost time. Don't think that it is too late to try.

No one has said that midlife will be easy. In fact, any midlife man who attempts a radical critique of his life will discover that there are parts of his personality that are heavily invested in maintaining the status quo. (If you've put twenty years into climbing the corporate ladder, it might be overwhelming to admit that you really don't even like the field you're in.) However, it has to be done. We need to reimagine our lives for our second half. We have to attempt to carve our own identity and find our unique place in the world. You did this before and made a few mistakes along the way (*as we all do*). Now you have a second chance to do it all over again, this time with so much more wisdom, fewer mistakes, and little regret.

A JOB WELL DONE

Reevaluating Our Work and

Careers at Midlife

~

BACKGROUND

AMERICA'S WORKFORCE IS rapidly changing and as baby boomers we are a large part of that change. Women are holding more professional jobs than ever before (while, of course, holding down their second—and third—jobs as nurses, chefs, and personal shoppers at home). With their success women are feeling their independence and physical and mental exhaustion. Men have essentially dominated the same jobs they always did, have lived by the same work ethic for generations, and have been treated with the same respect as always. Middle-aged men are used to waking up in the morning and going to work, coming home late and kissing the wife hello and the children goodnight. (Okay, what movie did that scene come from?) In reality, the picture is closer to this: both dad and mom wake up before dawn to check their e-mails, and head for the train while the kids head for school. (If they are empty-nesters then they might even have left before dawn to catch an hour at the gym; they do have to keep in shape and keep up with the younger generation who probably spent half the night on the treadmill.)

The bottom line is that by middle age you have worked a lot of years, and are ready to slow down. But how can you when the kids are in college, or you have to help your aging parents with the medical bills? The idea of saving for retirement becomes a fleeting thought. Suddenly midlifers find themselves restless and bored with their lives and their careers, but they are stuck. Their families are changing (and sadly, in so many cases, so are their spouses), they are squeezed between job demands and their personal lives, they are overwhelmed, stressed out, dissatisfied, and feeling trapped. The idea of making a midlife career change is frightening. There are so many negative stereotypes about older workers that most people over the age of forty might doubt if anyone would hire them. (It's a legitimate concern.) Technology is changing so rapidly that baby boomers have just caught on to teleconferencing and text messaging—and find they have to learn another language, as well (who knows if "IAM" means "I am *mad*" or "*miserable?*").

Earlier on, career choices were based on dreams, personal interest, market availability, and geographic location. You could do anything and live anywhere. At midlife the only career change that seems possible is retirement, whether voluntary or not. Although that may be the way you see it—it is not necessarily the truth. Midlife is a time to re-evaluate what work is meaningful to you and what works with your life. You have the experience to bring knowledge and wisdom to the table (which is something those twenty- and thirty-something's don't have.) Ageism does exist, but it doesn't have to keep you from making a career change.

The Office Is Not Where I Live:
Understand Why You Are Feeling the Way You Do

With maturity comes a confidence and the ability to redefine your work identity: the midlife search for meaning drives women into other pursuits; many change careers to find work that is more altruistic or fulfilling, or decide to go back to school. But that doesn't mean we don't have stress concerning our careers. The following are some common symptoms of general career-related stress.

Symptoms

FEELINGS

- You feel overworked and overwhelmed and are afraid of losing your job
- You feel burned out from longer hours and the effort to handle workplace challenges
- You are feeling squeezed between the demands of your own job, expectations of company leaders, and the desire to help managers and employees cope
- You have an overwhelming feeling of apathy and may become quiet or withdrawn
- You feel guilty about setting boundaries and limits; and about saying "No"
- You feel intimidated by younger workers
- You feel drained and that you have nothing more to give

THOUGHTS

- You experience cynicism and confusion about your job and coworkers
- You want to reduce stress and maintain harmony in key areas of your life
- You feel that your work life and personal life are out of balance
- You want to quit, change jobs, or retire early

BEHAVIOR

- You demonstrate a lack of caring or concern
- You spend more time at work than at home and you miss out on a rewarding personal life
- You exhibit poor work performance as a result of personal problems
- You struggle with juggling the demands of career and personal life
- You miss out on important family events
- You don't spend as much time with your friends

PRESENTING PROBLEMS

This Was Not in My Job Description: Overworked and Overloaded

You are getting older and work seems to be getting harder. Shouldn't it be the other way around, you get older and life gets easier? We have been made to believe that midlife is a time to slow down and think about retirement. But who has time for that when all you can think about is the amount of work you have to do, and that your coworker (fifteen years your junior) is waiting in line for your job? The more you are stressed the less productive you are and the less the boss likes you. (If you're lucky enough to be the boss, then it's the less that your employees like you.) Baby boomers like to turn every bad feeling into something positive: "multitasking" just means being overworked, overwhelmed, and having too much for one human to do.

Once you recognize what job stress can do to you—especially at midlife when you should be taking extra care of your health—something must be done. If stress is not managed, it can affect your physical and emotional health, relationships, and on-the-job performance. Common physical and emotional symptoms of stress include difficulty sleeping, headaches, irritability, anger, and mood swings. Burnout is an advanced effect of stress; a gradual process that seems to creep up on you and makes you feel detached from work and other significant roles and relationships. If you choose to ignore it and it becomes excessive and prolonged, it will cause mental, physical, and emotional strain. The result is lowered productivity, cynicism, and confusion, and a feeling of being drained and having nothing more to give—to your family, job, or yourself. You have choices to make—and most of these can be done without changing your job, or giving up all that your parents paid for your four, six, ten year degree.

You can reduce environmental stressors in the workplace and/or change your response to this stress. If after assessing the situation you determine that the workplace situation is unchangeable, and the toll it is taking on you is too great, then seeking options of other employment should be considered. Changing jobs for the right reason is nothing to be ashamed of and may lead to a much healthier situation in the long run.

The following self-assessment will help you determine the best course of action for you.

Confront, Compromise, and Change

- **Confront:** Assess what it is about your current position that you don't like: Is it the commute, your schedule, your salary, a coworker, or boss you just can't stand? Come up with a solution that you feel is reasonable and present it to whoever can make that change happen for you. (*You don't like the commute? Ask human resources about being relocated to another branch closer to home.*)
- **Compromise:** If you presented a solution that just didn't work, then include a compromise in the next solution. If they won't transfer you to the New York branch, what about the Connecticut branch? (*It still beats the commute from Pennsylvania.*)
- **Change:** If you have made attempts to confront and compromise but feel that you have gotten nowhere, and it is still is too much for you, and your health is suffering, well, you just might have to change jobs or careers.

Understanding and identifying the causes and effects of workplace stress is important for developing strategies for change. The critical component of any stress management program is the belief that alternatives exist. Feeling trapped and without choices is perhaps the greatest stressor of all.

Is This Is All Just a Waste of Time?

So you've worked hard for most of your life until now and look back and think: "All those years just for a paycheck? Did I really ever like that job? What was I thinking and why didn't I quit years ago when I was young?

(You know why: children to feed, tuition bills to pay, the golf membership, the car payments . . .)." We live in a society where people are encouraged to pursue careers based on money, status, power, and prestige, as opposed to one that brings self-fulfillment. So it really isn't your fault. Our parents encouraged us to do this because they wanted us to live better than them: education first, then a good job, and you are on your way to a good life. At midlife, we have the chance to find a more fulfilling career, but many of us rely on a variety of excuses for not doing so: We don't want to disrupt our lifestyle, change our routine, or lower our standard of living. So as a result we would rather be rich and unhappy. (After all, we promised the mortgage company we would earn six figures for at least the next thirty years, and who is going to pay for the kids' college, the senior ski vacation in Tahoe, or scuba lessons in Miami if we don't save now?)

The reality is that—despite getting stressed and worrying over every detail of our careers—we can find another job. Everyone is good at many jobs, and many jobs are good for many people. Remember that being unhappy at work will only make you unhappy in life. Look at how you are behaving and see if your dissatisfaction with your career is just a phase, the result of a bad day, or the result of a bad career choice you made years ago. We all have bad days at work but when you notice yourself performing your job grudgingly, using excessive sick leave, and displaying a bad attitude, these are signs that you're having a job or career crisis. If you find yourself identifying with these problems, take a closer look at your job, yourself, and your life and decide whether you should do something else that you would find fulfilling and satisfying. Only you can make the decision to take control of your life and switch to a more fulfilling career. But, before taking on the challenge of a career transition, become educated about what your other options are, and gather all the support from others that you can.

When Can I Get a Life?: Maintaining the Work/Life Balance

We think that by midlife we have worked hard and should feel the rewards. But in reality, most of us just feel confused, frustrated, and perhaps even angry. As we look back at our lives, and look forward to "what is left," the things we missed out on are the clearest to us. Perhaps we missed our child's graduation because we were in Paris closing a deal, or maybe we never saw our son's first home run. Maybe you thought you were doing it all for them and they would understand. But they don't, and they look back with the same regret that you weren't there. Finding a work-life balance in today's frenetically paced world is no simple task. But spend more time at work than at home and you miss out on a rewarding personal life.

Midlife is a time to slow down and spend time on things and with people that are important to you. Your aging parents won't be around much longer, and your kids have already left the nest. Thanksgiving and Christmas breaks will only last a few years, and the family vacations together become few and far between. But you are really caught in a vise. When your work life and your personal life are out of balance, stress and its harmful effects can take their toll. Take control, and consider how the world of work has changed, then reevaluate your relationship to work, and apply these strategies for striking a more healthy balance.

Try to Strike the Best Work/Life Balance

It isn't easy to juggle the demands of career and personal life. For most people, reducing stress and maintaining harmony in key areas of their life is a struggle.

Check and Balance Yourself:

- Know what time your job is over. (*At the very latest it should be when you walk in the door of your house . . . if not, just stay at the office until you are done.*)
- Eliminate or delegate activities you don't enjoy, don't have time for, or do only out of guilt. (*Ask someone else to order the flowers for the boss's anniversary—just make sure to tell them what their favorite flowers are.*)
- Find out what options your employer offers to make your life easier: flex hours, job-sharing, or telecommuting. (*If they don't, suggest it; no harm in asking. Some companies reward initiative.*)

- Manage your time. Organize your household and work-place efficiently. (*Remember there are only twenty-four hours in a day, and you should be sleeping for at least six of those.*)
- Refuse to take the guilt trip. It is okay for men and women to factor in their personal and family responsibilities. (*Everyone is entitled to have a sick parent, or a family wedding once in a while.*)
- Unplug your office connection. Turn the cell phone off, shut the computer, and step back from the office. (*You are only human, and need to mingle with humans outside the office.*)
- Take time off—especially if it is your day off. Don't accept phone calls, don't check your e-mail, and don't think about your JOB. (*Remember: The company did exist before they hired you and will stay in business until you get back.*)

Yes, the Problem Really Is My Job: Too Much Work, Not Enough Pay, and Other Midlife Gripes

You think your boss is great until you don't get the raise or the account you were promised. Hey, you are one of the seniors, and have worked at the company long enough: you deserve more. Sometimes in midlife we just have too many obligations to meet that keep us tied to our jobs. So we are stuck, but that doesn't mean we have to be miserable.

There are choices: you can spend hours planning the company's demise, or let the air out of your bosses' tires on his BMW. Or you accept the status quo and endure somehow until retirement. A better way to deal with these problems is to change your attitude about work and view it as just that: work, a J-O-B. Try to find other challenges and activities that fulfill you in other ways. Once you stop defining yourself by the job you have, the position you hold, or the career you have chosen, you will be much freer to accept the things at work that cause you so much discontent. We are really just people doing a job, and the job we do is secondary to who we really are in life.

However, the situation at your job may just be "unfixable." If that is the case, you may be ready for a career change.

One Strike and You are Out: Job Loss

No one has to remind you that you are getting old. Yet, with age discrimination, job layoffs, and downsizing, it seems like our age group is the first to "go" and the last to be hired. Of course they can pay the younger, less experienced worker a lower salary (and we can say, begrudgingly, "You get what you pay for"). The fear of getting fired or laid off looms over every worker's head, but it is the middle-aged worker who may fear it the most. It isn't easy to lose your job at any age, but at twenty or thirty you can still be confident that you will find another job. Many job searching Americans over forty encounter something called a "gray ceiling." It's the generation X (or those echo kids), that create a workforce barrier that is difficult for middle-aged workers to penetrate. Despite laws prohibiting it, most executives believe age discrimination in the workplace has increased during the past five years. No one will admit it—but it exists.

At midlife, many employers feel that you are "over the hill" and they still believe the common misconceptions and stereotypes that older workers are less productive than younger ones. Actually, numerous studies and research have shown that older workers' productivity rises due to greater dependability, better judgment, and improved accuracy. These studies show that older workers actually miss less work than younger workers and can learn new techniques and technologies effectively. Despite that, these "feel good" figures will be of little help if you have lost your job.

However, like any other disastrous event in your life, a job loss can present an opportunity for growth. The initial shock of a job loss may be enough to put you into a full-blown depression, and actually could be a mixed blessing. Think about the advantages that a midlife career change can bring (*Yes, there are some.*): You can find work that is less stressful and more meaningful; you can use skills and talents that you have developed over the years, ones you did not have when you were in your twenties or thirties; and you don't have to stay at your new job forever (retirement is not that far away). Make your age an asset next time around.

I'm That Old Already?: Age Discrimination and Baby Boomers

As our generation ages, we can expect to experience an uphill battle in our job search: Too many highly paid baby boomers are competing for the most competitive jobs (actually, *Fortune* magazine titled one recent issue's cover story, "Finished at Forty"). And while professionals in middle age are far from ready to retire, climbing the corporate ladder isn't for everyone. (Especially not for middle-aged people with bad backs.) For many, the greater levels of stress—competition and time commitment that go with high-level jobs—aren't worth the increase in power and pay. If that describes you, you may need to readjust your job-search strategies or career goals to compete in today's job market. Meanwhile, many older workers continue to live in a state of paranoia. Many older workers cite age discrimination and declining technology skills as the biggest reasons for not leaving the workforce today. The following will help you to make age an asset, not an obstacle, in your search.

MAKE AGE AN ASSET

Anticipate stereotypes and prepare to counter them: Make it clear in your cover letter and interviews that you're willing and able to adapt and have much to bring to the company. (*Don't forget to mention your maturity and reliability.*) Get tech-savvy: Update your cyber and computer skills; and break the misconception that older workers are inept and afraid of new technology. (*Hey, pull out your iPhone, download a few songs, and text a few messages to prove you know what you are doing.*)

INSIGHT

WORK LIFE IS just that: your life at work. The problem is that by midlife our jobs and careers have become an all-consuming obsession causing many to look back at their careers with regret—and to look forward to the years left with contempt. As we in midlife lament many of the mistakes we made, and ponder the many lessons along the way, we wonder why we were so driven toward material wealth and status. (Okay, we blame our parents for everything else, why not this?) I will tell you why: because at the time you made that early career decision you were old enough to follow your own dreams, and smart enough to recognize your own talents, and marketable enough to jump on the bandwagon to a better life (the one that justified that huge college tuition, actually). Now in midlife it has paid off: You probably have a great job; and a great house and car—and definitely wonderful kids. (And you're still asking yourself if you have a great life?)

So many changes happen in your life during the midlife years that you have to draw the line somewhere. Everything seems out of balance. But are you really going to tell your kids, "Enough change, no one moves out of the house to go to college"? Of course not. Just as, in the end, you'll (grudgingly) change your schedule for the umpteenth time to take your aging parent to the hospital; you'll resist the urge to tell the bank that you're burnt out from your job and will be taking a few months off from paying the mortgage, and so on. Instead, you stay with the job so you don't have to disrupt your lifestyle, change your routine, or lower your standard of living. And that's okay (for now).

In the back of your mind you fear that you will be laid off—and will never be able to find another job at your age. That's a legitimate fear but losing a job is not the end of the world. You have developed skills and talents throughout your life and your career that will be marketable. It may not be as easy as when you were thirty, but you do have some advantages. The stress of worrying about losing your job, along with the stress of dealing with the dissatisfaction with your present job, can make you literally sick. Remember, you just went on a low-cholesterol diet, are working out every day, and cutting out caffeine; so why would you let work give you a heart attack?

Try to figure out what really matters to you at this point of your career and life. (That is why you picked up the book in the first place, right?) Are you focused on those things, or are you going full-speed ahead in the opposite direction? Keep in mind that your job is more important than you think. No matter what you are doing in life, this is true: believe it or not, you can improve the world a little bit in every interaction you have and every role you play—if you decide you want to. Rediscover the deeper meaning for your work, and ask yourself, "How can I make someone's day?" and "How can I make my day?".

For just one day, instead of asking, "What will my job do for me today?" ask, "What can I give to work today?". One guaranteed way to lose your enthusiasm at work is to stop learning. Try identifying one small piece of your job that you want to improve and make that the part of the job you care about. Try new and creative ways to do what you have been doing for years. Whether you are in a career that needs renewing or undergoing a career change, you may feel that you are close to being done. But this time of life should be about *reclaiming* the joy of achievement and believing that what we do matters. Be appropriately assertive and don't feel guilty about setting boundaries and limits; say no when necessary. Recognize that stressful situations often result from someone else's inefficiency and tendency to manage by reactive crisis techniques rather than proactive postures. Someone I don't know once said: "The day you find a job you love will be the last day you ever work again." Think about and believe it. It's true.

MOVING FORWARD

BACKGROUND

*I*T SOUNDS PRETTY grim: gray hair, sagging eyelids, blue moods, aging parents, no more babies, and poor eyesight. No wonder we look in the mirror and long for our youth (or at least for a good plastic surgeon), and wonder where the years went. With the kids gone, and our parents' failing health, we begin to feel there has to be more to life than just caring for everybody else. After long climbs up the corporate ladder, late nights of waiting for our teenagers to come home, middle of the night calls from the nursing home, years of listening to our husbands snore, and hot flashes—we are exhausted. (And there's no denying that we are definitely older.) But one big upside is that we are definitely wiser.

The changes in midlife cause us to take a good look at where we have been, and make us think hard about where we are going. This reassessment can lead to a more compassionate attitude, richer emotional life, and a deepening of personal relationships. I know you are probably saying: *Like my life up to this point hasn't been compassionate? Hello, who buried the hamster and held their daughter's hand all night as she cried? And how much more emotional do I need to get than crying thirty-six hours down Interstate 95 after moving my child into their first dorm? Why would I want to do that now? Everyone I have ever had a deep relationship with* my whole life is leaving, or has already left me: the kids, my parents, perhaps my spouse, and even my friends are moving to Arizona to retire. From that point of view, it's easy to feel that way. But if you can look at midlife as an opportunity for freedom and independence you might feel a little better. Let's face it: Freedom is something that you haven't had in years; since your first job, your first (or only) wedding, or since the birth of your first child.

Midlife is a chance to start over again. You can redo the mistakes of your youth. You can become the person that you were meant to be, not the person you were expected to be. If you want to go back to school and become the actress you had always dreamed of being—go ahead. If you wished you could have learned to play the piano no one is stopping you (and actually, there are less people in the house to complain about your practicing). By midlife you have given so much to your families, and now you have the chance to reach out to the world and start fresh. If you love your dog as much as you tell everyone you do, go volunteer at the humane society. You can contribute to a cause or a charity and leave your own legacy to the next generation. (I know you already did that by having your kids . . . and they *are* the next generation and will benefit from whatever you contribute to the world now.)

Positive Symptoms (Actually, you might not even recognize yourself.)

THOUGHTS, FEELINGS, AND BEHAVIORS

- You are feeling grounded, independent, and satisfied
- You experience high levels of personal achievement
- You have greater ego resiliency—the ability to flexibly and resourcefully cope with stressors
- You have greater levels of satisfaction
- You have gained wisdom
- You have found freedom
- You are more independent
- You no longer have to put the needs of others first
- You can travel
- You can experiment and try new things

Freedom to Grow and to Go

Freedom can be hard to get used to. (It's not that you have exactly been in prison for the past twenty years, even if it felt like it when you were snowed in with the kids for three days.) So now that the kids are out of the house and you don't have anyone to make breakfast for, or to drive to school, or to fight with over what they are wearing—what do you do with yourself?

Start by making a list. Not of things you need to do around the house, or things you have ignored for years (like cleaning out your kids' closet), but things that you want to do for you. It is not unusual if you feel extreme guilt with each thing that you write down. You might consider "going to the gym after work instead of getting up at 5 AM." But then the guilt sets in: *no one will be home to make my husband dinner.* Now is as good a time as any to start rethinking your priorities: Your husband is old enough to make dinner for himself, or he can choose to wait for you to get home from the gym, or (gasp) he can decide to cook for both of you. If you think about volunteering your time at the crisis center, more guilt sets in. *Volunteer at the crisis center? We have crises everyday here with our parents in the nursing home. Shouldn't I devote my time to their crises?* Remember the things that we do for our families and loved ones don't count as things we do for ourselves. By no means do I advocate stopping doing things for your family, but I do encourage you to take the free time you have and spend it on things you *want* to do.

Midlife allows us so many choices of things to do and ways to live our lives that sometimes we find it difficult to handle the freedom. Wake up at 6:00 AM, wake the kids at 6:30, drive to the bus at 7:30, pick up the kids at 3:00, and then to soccer at 4:00. When you think about how many years you have spent following everyone else's schedules, having a half-day to yourself now can be downright unsettling. Find out what works for you and begin by rearranging times and routines, and you will feel the difference: freedom. From there, the possibilities are endless. Think about it. Who may not like your new routine, but you?

You have probably wished for "peace and quiet" at least a million times during your childrearing years. Well, at first you might complain that your dream has come true. Your house is too quiet. You lived with the laughter and the noise (and what about the fighting, and loud music). How about this: Start playing your music. Why not; this is the time to move your life to the beat of a different drummer. Things like music and art and nature really do put you in touch with yourself and with the beauty around you that maybe you have ignored. (And how could you really look at the sunset at the beach when you were making sure that a jellyfish didn't sting one of the kids?)

Regardless of the course you take in dealing with midlife, remember there is much to be gained during these years. Losing some of the angst of youth can have a calming effect—and create a clearer vision of more important dimensions of yourself that are worth developing. Midlife is a time to realize you no longer have to worry about being conservative or compromising, and are free to be who you want to be, instead of trying to act out some role. Wisdom, freedom from putting the needs of others first, independence, new social networks, and greater strength and capacity are all possibilities.

Live a Little

- **Stay positive:** Look for the good in life. See life through new lenses. Be kind to others. It makes them feel good, and makes you feel good. And just play a little: What are the things that you have always wanted to do, but keep putting off? Writing the great American novel, learning to sail, planting a garden?

- **Give it a break:** Take time for you. Just a few ten-to fifteen-minute breaks each day can add happiness to your life. Do something special for yourself during those breaks: kiss your spouse, call a grandkid, or go for a walk—celebrate the small moments.

- **Let music sooth your soul:** Listen to music that makes you dance, sing, and laugh and that reminds you that you are alive.

- **Laugh a little:** Surround yourself with people who look at the lighter side of life, and when you're alone, go out of your way to look for opportunities to laugh.

- **Be grateful:** Stop and smell the roses. Look at the good you have in your life, and say Thanks.

Strengthening the Bond With Our Parents

Men and women find that middle age can be a time of intense deepening of relationships with friends and family. You finally understand your parents—and also, now that you have been in their shoes, they are less "magically omnipotent." You realize that they really didn't know everything like you thought they did growing up. (We should have gotten the clue when we realized they were never ten feet tall.) In a sense, they almost become your peers. As parents grow older and die, however, we may idealize them once more. We gradually forgive them for their shortcomings, since we can no longer secretly hope for them to change or amend earlier mistakes. As people grow older, they tend to see their parents as having done their best, and largely forgive them for their real limitations and mistakes.

A Work in Progress: Becoming Your Own, Improved Person

From childhood on we carry with us scripts of the "shoulds" and "should nots" that we have learned as children. We hear our parents', teachers', and preachers' voices in every decision we make. Oftentimes we have struggled to do the right thing. As our parents age and pass on, we sometimes feel a sense of freedom to act as we always wanted to. We realize that they are not there to judge or criticize us, or be hurt by our decisions. It is not easy to break this script, or change our perception of ourselves and our capabilities. Your identity for so many years has been tied into the roles you have played and the scripts you have followed that it sometimes is difficult to figure out who you really are.

At midlife people often look deep inside themselves to find answers to their unhappiness, struggles, or regrets. (Really, who had any time over the last twenty years to think about anything but which kid needed to be picked up at what time?) This search usually results in a greater under-standing of life and a greater compassion for others. Whether you look for it or not, you will most likely find the good within yourself, and feel a new obligation to share that with others. Don't get me wrong: we don't all emerge from midlife as saints and crusaders—but we do realize that in many ways we are fortunate and have been selfish. We think how lucky we have been to have a good job while others are homeless. If we hated our jobs we feel fortunate that we have enjoyed good health while others are suffering. And as we recognize our special and unique talents we need to find ways to share them with others. The bottom line is that if we can find the good in ourselves, we will have an easier time grappling with the meaning of life, and in making a plan for the second half of our lives.

Recognize that as we get older, we have the potential to get better. In the first half of life you develop one idea of who you think you are. At midlife, we focus on becoming who we were meant to be rather than who we think others want us to be. We examine and evaluate every aspect of our lives and search for deeper meaning. Remember to put your ego in its place. If your habitual thoughts are trying to take over, tell them to take a back seat. You can try saying, "You made your point, now go away" (although you might want to practice this when no one is around). Then move on and don't fight or struggle with your ego. Keep your thoughts and feelings focused on joy and your inner connection to spirit.

No Better Time Than Now: Enjoy the Abundances of Midlife

It's okay to be selfish. After years of nurturing and caring for others, you have earned the right to put yourself first. It's perfectly fine to have a facial, travel by yourself, or have a relationship without a wedding ring. Chances are you'll find out that almost everything gets better after fifty (okay, maybe not your figure). Midlife is a time when many women come into their own, feeling grounded, independent, and satisfied with what they have. Many women actually enjoy moving into middle age, and experience increased levels of personal achievement and a new sense of adventure as parenting roles and other duties subside.

We all deserve to live a rich, rewarding life. When we start to feel down

motivated about the direction our life is taking, it's time to explore
v avenues of personal growth and development. More and more
people don't see midlife as a crisis but instead see it as a challenge—and
even an opportunity.

INSIGHTS

IF YOU TALK to anyone who is going through midlife or has
already been through it, they will tell you it wasn't fun at
first. But once they got into the swing of it, it ended up being
better fun than they expected. If you ask them what they like
best now that the kids are grown up and moved out, they'll
often joke, "I can walk around naked." But the significance
of this common response is that it symbolizes the freedom
that midlife adults have to do anything they want to do. With
middle age comes the freedom to live life the way you have
dreamed it. Don't be afraid of the freedom you are given.
Don't regret your past. Just change your future. Don't imagine
what this next stage in life will be; but plan for it, and live
it. If you think everything was so great when you were in your
twenties, think again. In reality, there was plenty of good and
plenty of struggles. You had tight abs then, and a full head of
hair—but you probably didn't have the security you have now,
and certainly not the maturity.

Feeling restless, discontented, and lost causes people in midlife
to seek an answer, make a change, and do something different
with their lives so they can return to a balanced state of harmony.
Still others just want some inner peace, after years of struggle.
They are older and tired of being discontented. They realize that
this is their last chance for a second journey. Others have waited
and planned their whole life for retirement, but never lived their
life along the way. Once midlife hits they are ready for change.

Some midlife adults are prepared to change, but don't always know how. They can feel and can see that they are different (and so can everyone else, but are afraid to tell them). Their journey of transformation is one that only they can figure out.

If you're reading this, you know what it feels like: the restlessness, the desire to be younger and to do all the things you did when you were twenty-one. This phase of life leads some to take up windsurfing and others to go for plastic surgery, some to exercise regimens and still others to leave their spouses. In a sense this is the "grass is always greener on the younger side" stage of life. This is when we ask ourselves questions like: "Why can't we all get better looking with age, like Patrick Dempsey, Julia Roberts, or Demi Moore? How can I get my twenty-year-old body back? I've only got a few good years left, why stick it out in this same old rut?" I've seen people leave perfectly good spouses to set off for greener pastures, only to find those pastures sparser than the ones they left behind. Remember: Midlife is about reclaiming your youth—and you don't have to turn your entire world upside down to feel young. And it doesn't have to be a problem time in your life, either. There are many things you can do to gain a more positive attitude about maturing and to affirm midlife.

If you feel yourself getting depressed about getting older, seek out and speak with an older friend. You can gain comfort, wisdom, and some humorous insight if you give these conversations time. Whatever you do, don't become paralyzed with fear. Even though it seems like everything you once counted on seems to be gone, don't give in. Try to gain a new perspective: What you are going through is normal, and temporary. You will see better days, and you can emerge a better person, as well.

Resist the urge to run from everything. Sure, you can hide behind an extramarital affair, drinking too much, or by shutting out your loved ones, but these "solutions" are only temporary, and are more trouble than they are worth. Finally, don't give in. We must take this time to come to terms with our past, figure out what is important to us, and begin moving forward. The only restrictions you have are when you stop seeing the wonderful possibilities life has to offer you, at any age.

Go say you are sorry to your sister, your brother; work on your relationship with your spouse. Spend time with your family and friends or actually make new friends. This is a time in your life that you can get rid of the emotional baggage that you have carried along for so long, and travel lightly through this second part of your journey.

BIBLIOGRAPHY

Adler, Gerhard and R.F.C. Hull trans. and eds. *The collected works of C.G. Jung.* Vol. 6: Psychological types (Herbert Read, Michael Fordham, Gerhard Adler, & William McGuire, Eds.)

American Psychiatric Association (2000). (DSM-IV-TR) "Diagnostic and statistical manual of mental disorders," 4th edition, text revision. Washington, DC: American Psychiatric Press, Inc.

Beck Aaron, T., M.D. *Love is Never Enough: How Couples Can Overcome Misunderstandings, Resolve Conflicts, and Solve Relationship Problems Through Cognitive Therapy.* Harper & Row, 1988.

Blakeslee, Sandra and Judith S. Wallerstein. *The Good Marriage: How And Why Love Lasts.* Houghton Mifflin Company, 1995.

Cohen, Gene D. PhD. *The Mature Mind: The Positive Power of the Aging Brain.* Basic Books, 2007.

Crittenden, Ann. *The Price of Motherhood: Why the Most Important Job in the World Is Still the Least Valued.* Metropolitan Press, 2001.

Ellis, Albert, Ph.D. *How to Stubbornly Refuse to Make Yourself Miserable About Anything: Yes, Anything!* Carol Publishing Group, 1995.

Erikson, Erik H., ed. *Adulthood.* W. W. Norton, 1978.

Etaugh, Claire A. and Judith S. Bridges, *The Psychology of Women: A Lifespan Perspective.* Allyn and Bacon, 2001.

Hoffman, Lois. *Mothers at Work: Effects on Children's Well-Being* (Cambridge Studies in Social and Emotional Development). Cambridge University Press, 1999.

Hunter, Ski, Sundel, Sandra S., Sundel, Martin. *Women at Midlife: Life Experience and Implications for the Helping Professions.* Washington: National Association of Social Workers, 2002.

Kubler-Ross, Elisabeth. *Death: The Final Stage of Growth.* Prentice-Hall, 1975.

Margulies, Sam, PhD., J.D. *Getting Divorced Without Ruining Your Life: A Reasoned, Practical Guide to the Legal, Emotional and Financial Ins and Outs of Negotiating a Divorce Settlement.* Simon and Schuster, 1992.

Nolen-Hoeksema, Susan PhD. *Women Who Think Too Much: How to Break Free of Overthinking and Reclaim Your Life.* Owl Books, 2004.

Sheehy, Gail. *New Passages: Mapping Your Life Across Time.* New York, NY: The Ballentine, 1995.

Sheehy, Gail. *Passages: Predictable Crises of Adult Life.* New York: Dutton, 1976.

Wilcox, Susan, Ph.D. "The Effects of Widowhood on Physical and Mental Health, Health Behaviors and Health Outcomes: The Women's Health Initiative." American Psychological Association, Inc., 2003.

Youngblade, Lise M. and Lois Hoffman. *Mothers at Work: Effects on Children's Well-Being.* Cambridge University Press, 1999.

⅃l References

⼂in, Carolyn M. and Michael R. Levenson, University of California at Davis. "Stress, Coping, and Health at Midlife: A Developmental Perspective." Handbook for Midlife Development by Maggie E. Lachman 2002, Wiley Publisher.

Banister, E. M. (2000). "Women's midlife confusion: Why am I feeling this way?" Issues in Mental Health Nursing, 21, 745–764, December 2000.

Cash, Thomas F. and Patricia E. Henry. "Women's body images: The results of a national survey in the U.S.A." Sex Roles, Vol. 33, 1995.

Chandler, Carol and Joyce Fittro. "Enhancing Midlife Marriage." Ohio State University Extension, 2002.

Chase, Mark H. "Counseling re-entry Women: An Overview Journal of Employment." Counseling Alexandria: Dec. 2002 Vol. 39, Issue 4, p 146–152.

Hurst, S. R. and M. W. Wiederman. "Physical attractiveness, body image, and women's sexual self-schema," Psychology of Women Quarterly, 21, 567–580, (1997).

Mahoney, Sarah. "Baby Boomers Value Caring For Aging Parents More Than Earlier Generation." Article Date: 05 Dec 2006 (Article adapted by Medical News Today from original press release.) AARP, The Magazine: The Secret Lives of Single Women, May & June 2006.

Sheehy, Gail. "On surviving the unpredictable." Program and abstracts of the 5th Annual Meeting of the National Association. of Nurse Practitioners in Women's Health; September 25–28, 2002; Scottsdale, Arizona.

Sloan, Bridgette. "Body Image." Fact Sheet, Extension Agents, Family and Consumer Sciences/Community Development, Ohio State University, HYG 5238–00.

Stern, Steven and Tennille J. Checkovich. "Shared Care-giving Responsibility of Adult Siblings with Elderly Parents." Journal of Human Resources, Vol. 37, No. 3, June 2002.

Online References

Clay, Rebecca A., "Researchers replace midlife myths with facts." APA Online, Monitor on Psychology Volume 34, No. 4 (April 2003) http://www.apa.org/monitor/apr03/researchers. html (Accessed December 15th, 2007) Print version: page 36.

Jacoby, Susan. "Sex in America," AARP The Magazine, July & August, 2005, http://www. aarpmagazine.org/lifestyle/relationships/sex_in_america.html (Accessed—December 15th, 2007).

Mayo Clinic Staff, Mayo Clinic. "Work-life balance: Ways to restore harmony and reduce stress." (Jun 1, 2006). http://www.mayoclinic.com/health/work-life-balance/WL00056.

National Survey of Midlife Development in the United States (MIDUS) online at http://midmac. med.harvard.edu/research.html#res1.

Ohio State University Extension Senior Series. "When Does Someone Attain Old Age?" For more information, visit the Ohio Department of Aging web site at: http://www.state.

oh.us/age/ and Ohio State University Extension's "Aging in Ohio" web site at: http://www. hec.ohio-state.edu/famlife/aging/index.htm.

US Census Bureau, Special Edition, January 3, 2006 "Oldest Baby Boomers Turn 60!" http://www. census.gov/PressRelease/www/releases/archives/facts_for_features_special_editions/006105. html (Accessed—December 15th, 2007)

MENTAL HEALTH RESOURCES AND REFERRALS

AMERICAN ASSOCIATION OF RETIRED PERSONS (AARP)

www.aarp.org/internetresources/
601 E Street, NW
Washington, D.C. 20049

Database of Internet resources and links to hundreds of sites for people age 50+.

AMERICAN PSYCHIATRIC ASSOCIATION

www.healthyminds.org
1000 Wilson Boulevard
Suite 1825
Arlington, VA, 22209

Healthy Minds Healthy Lives is a resource for mental health information and news through its web site Healthy Minds Healthy Lives. The public can access up-to-date information on individual and family mental health needs, resources, and referrals.

AMERICAN PSYCHOLOGICAL ASSOCIATION

www.apahelpcenter.org
750 First Street, NE
Washington, D.C. 20002

The Help Center is a resource for brochures, tips, and articles on the psychological issues that affect physical and emotional well-being. Information about referrals to mental health professionals is available.

MAYO CLINIC

www.mayoclinic.com/health/mental-health/MH99999

13400 East Shea Blvd.
Scottsdale, AZ 85259

The site contains information on mental health and mental illness, specific disorders and mental health treatments. Strategies to improve individuals' personal mental health are also included.

Other address:

San Pablo Road
Jacksonville, FL 32224

and

200 First St. S.W.
Rochester, MN 55905

MENTAL HEALTH AMERICA

www1.nmha.org/infoctr/factsheets/
12.cfm

Mental Health America's fact sheet "Finding the Right Care" provides detailed information to help patients choose a therapist and enable them to better understand treatment options and the treatment process.

NATIONAL INSTITUTE OF MENTAL HEALTH

www.nimh.nih.gov

U.S. DEPARTMENT OF HEALTH AND HUMAN SERVICES

6001 Executive Boulevard, Room 8184, MSC 9663
Bethesda, MD 20892–9663

The "For the Public Section" provides information on symptoms, diagnosis, and treatment of mental disorders, and other educational materials.

NATIONAL WOMEN'S HEALTH INFORMATION CENTER

www.womenshealth.gov/
200 Independence Avenue, S.W.
Washington, D.C. 20201
Women's health resources and materials for consumers and professionals, sponsored by the U.S.

SAMHSA'S NATIONAL MENTAL HEALTH INFORMATION CENTER

www.mentalhealth.samhsa.gov/cmhs/
P.O. Box 42557
Washington, D.C. 20015
Links users to the Federal efforts to treat mental illnesses, promote mental health, and prevent the development or worsening of mental illness.

HELP LINES

The National Suicide Prevention Lifeline's 2-hour toll-free crisis hotline, 1-800-273-TALK (1-800-273-8255), can put you into contact with your local crisis center that can tell you where to seek immediate help in your area.

In areas where 211 is available, dialing this number can connect you with mental health crisis services in your area or help you find where to seek immediate help in your area.

OTHER SUGGESTED RESOURCES

- Your local health department's Mental Health Division
- Family physician
- Clergyperson
- Family Social services agencies
- Educational consultants or school counselors
- Marriage and family counselors
- Psychiatric hospitals (accredited by the Joint Commission on Accreditation of Health Care Organizations)
- Hotlines, crisis centers, and emergency rooms (call 411 for Directory Assistance)

DISCLAIMER NOTICE

While these resources can be helpful, specific concerns regarding the diagnosis and treatment of any mental disorders affecting yourself or a family member should be discussed with your healthcare provider. The information contained in these web sites is not intended as, and is not a substitute for, professional medical advice. All decisions about clinical care should be made in consultation with a qualified health care professional. The author is not responsible for content provided on these websites and does not guarantee the accuracy of the information they contain.